SEEDS OF WISDOM

PROCEEDINGS OF THE 1996 UNDERGRADUATE PHILOSOPHY CONFERENCE

EDITED
BY

DOUGLAS W. SHRADER

ONEONTA PHILOSOPHY STUDIES
HISTORICAL AND CULTURAL PERSPECTIVES

10 9 8 7 6 5 4 3 2

ISBN 1-883058-08-2

Library of Congress Cataloging-in-Publication Data

Title: **Seeds of Wisdom**
Editor: Douglas W. Shrader
Subject: Philosophy

For

JOSEPH C. PITT

a friend whose example
has often provided inspiration

ONEONTA PHILOSOPHY STUDIES

HISTORICAL AND CULTURAL PERSPECTIVES

Department of Philosophy

SUNY-ONEONTA

Oneonta, NY 13820-4015

http://www.oneonta.edu/~shradedw/ops.html

CONTENTS

Historical Reflections

PREFACE

Each fall the SUNY-Oneonta Philosophy Department joins forces with faculty at Binghamton University, Dowling College, *et al* to cosponsor an international conference on Ancient and Medieval Philosophy. Now in its sixteenth year, the conference attracts hundreds of scholars from around the world. Participating organizations include the Institute of Global Cultural Studies (IGCS), International Society for Neoplatonic Studies (ISNS), Society for Ancient Greek Philosophy (SAGP), Society for Aristotelian Studies (SAS), Society for Global Africa (SGA), and Society for the Study of Islamic Philosophy and Science (SSIPS). Hosted in previous years by Baruch College and Columbia University, the conference is now generally held in Binghamton (about fifty miles from Oneonta).

In October of 1995, I invited students from my *Metaphysics* class to attend the conference. To my delight, they not only accepted my invitation but returned from the weekend with a level of enthusiasm and intellectual intensity that surpassed even my own idealistic projections. They simply could not stop talking about the presentations they had heard or the people they had met. Soon they were talking about having a conference of their own: *for students!* The Philosophy Club agreed to host the event; Dr. Achim Köddermann and I agreed to provide oversight and guidance. We selected a date, pieced together a patchwork of funding, and hoped for the best.

On March 16, 1996 our students' bold dream became a reality. Twenty undergraduates from seven institutions presented papers. Twenty others served as session chairs and/or commentators. Awards for top papers were presented to Jennifer Burke (Temple University), Michael Joseph (Oneonta), and Gabrielle Levin (Oneonta). The keynote address, "Imaginative Cosmology from Plato to Einstein", was provided by Thomas Robinson

(University of Toronto, President of the International Plato Society). To recognize the special role they played in organizing and hosting the conference, the Ninash Foundation presented East/West Awards to Kerri Nicholas and Alex Slater.

Despite a tight schedule and a shoestring budget, the conference was a rousing success. Presentations were clear, insightful, and informed. Discussion was spirited and robust. Selecting the top three papers was not easy. Nor was it easy to decide which papers to include in the present volume.

Following much discussion, the editorial board of Oneonta Philosophy Studies decided to publish a substantial, yet still highly selective proceedings. To be accepted for conference presentation, the papers had already been subjected to extensive, blind review. We could have published the full set of referred papers, as is common for conferences such as this, but decided that it was important to set a standard higher than the traditional norm. Hopefully, the result will speak for itself.

Though largely unintentional, the ten papers in this volume divide nicely into three sections:
Science, Metaphysics, and the Construction of Reality,
Philosophical Journeys of Self and Spirit, and
Historical Reflections.

In *Biological Research and Feminist Obligation*, Jennifer Burke explores the important but often misunderstood relationship between scientific research and socio-political values, focusing particularly on the views of Helen Longino and Helen Lambert. She skillfully analyzes the assumptions and implications of each position, outlines two models of theorizing about sex-differentiated behavior (per Longino), and ultimately argues that Longino's position is preferable to that of Lambert.

In *Subjective versus Objective Reality: An Examination Through Physics and Philosophy*, Michael Joseph tackles an age-old debate about the nature of perception and reality. Following a preliminary sketch of the issues, he presents, analyzes, and discusses three viewpoints: (i) Plato's theory of forms, (ii) the scientific ideal of Newtonian physics, and (iii) contemporary interpretations associated with quantum mechanics and relativity theory. Though clearly sympathetic to objective standards, Michael concludes: "Since all that can be understood, can be understood only through the human mind, which can alter and even create reality (as the new physics shows), reality itself must be subjective" (p. 29).

In *Exploring the Universe: From Plato to Einstein and Beyond*, Alex Slater continues the exploration begun by Michael Joseph in the preceding paper. Inviting us to use our imaginations to travel through time, he constructs a dialogue which involves Socrates, Plato, and Einstein. He explores Platonic cosmology, the nature of light, and the construction of a space-time matrix. In the final analysis, Alex opts for a view which unifies the cosmos, microcosm, and macrocosm in ways which defy not only some principal assumptions of modern physics, but his own imagination as well.

In *Observing, Observability, and the Importance of a Smiler: A Partial Defense of Strawsonian Events*, David Miguel Gray concludes this section with an insightful analysis of the complex conceptual and ontological relationships between events and objects. He distinguishes "weak" from "strong" dependencies, explores Strawson's views concerning event-object relations, and examines Moravcsik's criticisms of the Strawsonian picture. Based on his own analysis of dependency relationships, David argues that Moravcsik's criticism commits a category mistake and thereby fails to dispose of Strawson's basic particulars.

The second section of the text opens with an essay by Angela Case. In *Follow Your Bliss: The Philosophy of Joseph Campbell*, Angela examines the life, work, and beliefs of this famous professor of mythology. Through analysis of his work with hero myths and the practice of yoga, the essay demonstrates Campbell's belief that human life is a journey. Though initially a search for explanations, Angela argues that the journey can be transformed into a celebration of the mystery of life (which Campbell terms *bliss*).

In *Concepts of Self: East and West*, Gabrielle Levin examines the complex interactions between different Eastern cultures as they have influenced and been influenced by each other's definitions of self. She incorporates reflections from Buddhism, Confucianism, Taoism, Shinto, and Zen and traces the contributions of each tradition as the notion of self is filtered through the various cultures. Gabrielle concludes with speculations concerning the lessons which Western society could learn from Eastern society, and vice-versa.

In *Quality, Love, and Madness: Pirsig versus Plato*, Kerri Nicholas compares two classic journeys of self and spirit: Plato's *Phaedrus* and Robert Pirsig's *Zen and the Art of Motorcycle Maintenance*. She begins with a discussion of Pirsig's search for Quality, including his analysis of the Subjective/Objective dichotomy as well as the Classical/Romantic split. After arguing that "*Quality* is an unbounded term that can be used in many different ways" (page 108), Kerri turns to an examination of love and madness. Following Plato, she agrees that love is a form of madness but argues against both closure and obsession.

The third and final section of the text is inaugurated by John Devine's essay, *Nietzsche's Appropriative Representation* or *Is the Overman a Hermaphrodite?* We are invited to consider the relationship between Nietzsche's grandiose style of writing and the birth of the overman. John accepts themes of sexuality as a legitimate framework for discussing Nietzsche's style and writing, but rejects the specifics of Derrida's "heterocentric" reading. He opts instead for a "hermaphroditic" reading which "not only attempts to penetrate the text ... but allows that it should penetrate you" (page 126). Approached in this way, he argues, "Nietzsche gives us the possibility of a world which simply has sexuality and writing, which implores us to explore, to read, and more*over* to *live* through these activities" (page 127).

As his title suggests (*The Impossibilities, Irrationality, and Contradictions of Immanuel Kant's Ethical Theories*) David Schaaf is not impressed with Kant's approach to ethics. He presents and analyzes the key concepts of Kant's system, including the notion of a good will, the ideal of a categorical imperative, the concept of duty, and the conditions of ethical behavior. Through a series of examples, David details the basis of his disagreement with Kant. To further support his position, he provides a brief discussion of the views of John Stuart Mill and William David Ross.

In *Descartes and Nietzsche*, Tatiana Zelikina examines the multi-faceted role of philosophical tradition. Both Descartes and Nietzsche, she argues, represent cognitive revolutions. Both, in some sense, discredit the history of their own discipline to start anew. Interestingly, Tatiana's concern with Descartes' and Nietzsche's "implied readers" provides an intriguing link to John Devine's paper. Her analysis of Nietzsche's *On the Genealogy of Morals* connects well with David Schaaf's discussion of Kant's ethical theories.

Douglas W. Shrader
Oneonta, New York

ACKNOWLEDGEMENTS

The conference and this volume depend on the contributions and good will of many. Special appreciation is extended to:

SUNY-Oneonta Student Association for financial support

Ninash Foundation for financial support

Oneonta Philosophy Studies editorial board for financial support and manuscript review

Green Mountain Coffee for donating coffee

Eric Sloan and the Organization of Ancillary Services for catering the conference dinner

Tom Robinson for sacrificing his weekend to deliver the keynote address

Parviz Morewedge for his enthusiasm and technical assistance

Dan Bristol, Kerri Nicholas, David Schaaf, and Alex Slater for editorial assistance

SUNY-Oneonta administration for support and encouragement — especially Dean James Mullen, Provost Anne C. Federlein, and President Alan B. Donovan

IGCS, SAGP, and SSIPS for financial and in-house support of this series

Finally, a heartfelt **Thank You** is extended to all the Presenters, Chairs, and Commentators — for without them there would have been no Conference.

Science, Metaphysics, and The Construction of Reality

Biological Research and Feminist Obligation

Jennifer Burke
Temple University

Introduction

Critics of the biological sciences have noted the ways in which scientific research is both the effect and the cause of our socio-political values. Helen Longino[1] and Helen Lambert[2] have expressed concern representative of many philosophers of science about the implications of scientific studies for feminists and scientists (and feminist scientists): how do particular theories inscribe oppressive sensibilities, and how should scientifically and socio-politically responsible scientists negotiate theories with differing points of emphasis for biological and environmental factors in determining human behavior? While Longino and Lambert both wish for the advancement of human potential, their pragmatic assessment and conceptions of science's and scientists' responsibilities to this goal contrast sharply. This paper seeks to examine some of the socio-political ramifications of the biological sciences, and to argue for the superiority of Longino's position. Longino and Lambert, though identifying similar problems and possessing similar socio-political agendas, part ways in their prescriptions for pragmatic response. First, I will outline two paradigmatic models of theorizing the basis of sex-differentiated behavior as delineated by Longino, contrasting her views on science and its societal obligations with those of Lambert.

Two Models of the Basis of Sex-Differentiated Behavior

To demonstrate how extra-scientific, ideological commitments may influence theory construction and choice, Helen Longino juxtaposes two explanatory models of the biological basis of sex-differentiated behavior.[3] Through her analytically neutral perspective, Longino discusses the constitutive aspects[4] of the linear hormonal and selectionist models. Both models purport to explain gendered and/or sex-related behavior as a function of human neural organization and its relation to gonadal hormone exposure (either testosterone or female androgens) during the prenatal/perinatal period(s) of fetal development. Through her analysis of evidential relations in the hypotheses of the models, Longino indicates how the respective models further both an unstated ideological program with material and political consequences as well as a scientifically acceptable one. Specifically, she indicates how the contextual values[5], or assumptions, implicit in the linear hormonal model are tied to present structures of socio-economic oppression, whereas such values in the selectionist model correspond to a more egalitarian vision of human potential. To elaborate on Longino's concerns about the implications of each model's ideological character, both models require some brief delineation.

(1) The Linear-Analytic Model

As an exemplar of the linear-analytic explanatory framework,[6] Longino describes the linear hormonal model of causation that Anke Ehrhardt, in particular, employs in her research. Generally, the linear-analytic framework provides a deterministic account of a phenomenon in which a given result is traced to a sequence of fixed, isolable, independently-occurring biochemical events operating in an unalterably unidirectional manner; the consequences of a phenomenon, particularly sex-related behaviors, may be entirely outside the control of the individual. In this theory, Ehrhardt claims that gender role behaviors, such as "play behavior (indoor or outdoor), degree of 'parenting rehearsal,' and career preferences,"[7] are the result of exposure to gonadal hormones during the perinatal/prenatal period(s). Ehrhardt does allow "for the [weak] interaction of physiological and environmental factors":[8] she proposes that environmental factors may cause some hormonally-determined characteristics to become manifest instead of others.

As Longino and others have pointed out, this research incurs several problems on a scientific (constitutive) level. First, Ehrhardt does not account for the "degree of variability" from person to person "even within hormonal groups."[9] Next, the use of animal research provides very weak correlational evidence for Ehrhardt's claim; for example, animal experiments do not replicate "the complex social environments in which humans develop."[10] Moreover, variables usually found in human environments cannot be isolated as they can be in experiments involving the "single factor analysis"[11] that occurs in labs. Nor do all mammalian species possess similar organs: the human brain is "larger and more complex" than those of other primates.[12] Additionally, human behaviors "exhibit a degree of intentionality not characteristic"[13] of laboratory animals. Finally, the evidence is not specific enough to be convincing; for example, she provides no indication of what an environmental factor may be,[14] nor does she indicate "precisely the amount of hormone to which individuals were exposed."[15]

(2) The Selectionist Model

In contrast, the selectionist model, as espoused in the work of Vernon Mountcastle and Gerald Edelman, posits gender role and sex-related behaviors as the result of interaction between biological factors and cognitively self-determined states. On Mountcastle's and Edelman's accounts, neuronal groups arranged in vertical columns throughout the neocortex of the human brain both receive and send signals to other groups; one group may receive simultaneous signals from several groups and can respond to one or more of the signals in different ways.[16] Neural groups will form connections among themselves selectively in order to form repertoires, or "functional patterns."[17] First, primary repertoires develop through selections "based on function, in which certain connections stabilize and others vanish."[18] Next, secondary repertoires are selected from the primary ones; however, their selection, although similarly based on function, is determined "in response to experience."[19]

Hence, the secondary repertoires are perpetually re-adjusting in response to "intentional or voluntary behavior, which involves the representation of self, action, world, and the consequences of action to oneself."[20] The dynamic interaction of self and world in this model restores the individual's agency, and thus, his/her capacity for self-determination. Edelman also postulates "phasic reentry" through which continual representations exist and our awareness of them is possible.[21] Longino emphasizes in particular that as a result, "consciousness is less a property of the physical brain than a *process* [my emphasis] of the brain";[22] the processes described in this account are highly compatible with the feminist notion of a "person as a being capable of making and acting on intelligent [and self-determined] decisions."[23] This account permits for the interaction of not only "physiological and environmental factors but also for the interaction of these with a continuously self-modifying, self-representational (and self-organizing) central processing system."[24]

As does Ehrhardt's work, the selectionist research project possesses complications as well. Although evidence about the structuring of the brain on this account is compelling, work is still required to understand the molecular and cellular level of the "cellular adhesion" involved in the "development of neural networks."[25] More research is needed to understand the type of functional organization of the neocortex that creates primary and secondary repertoires.[26] The work of cultural anthropologists regarding "cultural variation in the expression of sex-differentiated behaviors" has not consistently supported this claim of such diversity in sex-differentiated behaviors across cultures;[27] Lambert also indicates that dimorphism, in fact, has been supported in "most cross-cultural studies [that] have described ... superior male performance on spatial tasks."[28] In addition, by virtue of this model's own epistemic points of emphasis, the selectionist theory "assumes the self-initiating, intentional character of human behavior" without indicating "what could count as empirical evidence" for this assertion.[29] Finally, critics have also noted that this model abandons the simplicity of the previous model.[30]

Longino's Perspective

In both the linear hormonal and selectionist theories, the correlational character of data is open to attack; in Longino's words, "Once the model is elaborated in a general way, it remains to show that it applies to humans."[31] Correlations make this leap to the human sphere through the mediation of explanatory frameworks. It is the strength of these correlations that gives a theory credibility and validity. As both Longino and Lambert indicate, these correlations may assume a highly ideological character that may not endanger a research project's constitutive status, but may perpetuate societal stereotypes that interfere with an individual's right to self-determination.

Longino phrases the dilemma: "Correlation after correlation is produced with no attempt to understand just what it is that is being measured or its relation to the associated phenomenon."[32] Correlations in hypotheses translate into a culture's attitudes about social equality, personhood (and conceptions of human nature) and political ideals[33] which, in turn, translate into how we determine the extent of an individual's rights and of justice. Given that two different research projects may meet the standards of empirical adequacy and other rules determining constitutive standards in a given sub-community of the scientific community,[34] how do we determine which is "better"? Should we take both theories as equally useful for understanding a phenomenon? Should extra-scientific concerns positively or negatively influence our attitude toward one theory over another?

Longino points out that "internal, evidential considerations alone are not sufficient to support one rather than the other."[35] Though weaknesses and strengths exist in the constitutive aspects of both Ehrhardt's and Mountcastle and Edelman's research projects, "the arguments for [a] model are not decisive," but "neither are these arguments against [a model] decisive."[36] On Longino's view, *one must choose a political stance and work to reconcile the demands of one's ideological commitments with the standards of one's scientific community.* Thus, when the constitutive aspects of two theories can no longer guide us to a choice between them, *then our consciously-examined contextual values should lead us to choose the more desirable theory — the theory that is most likely to permit social change and progress toward democratic, egalitarian ideals.* For example, Ehrhardt's work, in Longino's formulation, translates vaguely into support for traditional roles — whether in implicitly permitting teachers to allow boys to get away with less self-discipline and greater physical expressiveness or to encourage girls to be quiet and more domestically oriented.[37]

On the other hand, the selectionist theory situates self-representation, self-determination and the resultant decision-making process under the control of the individual; if the nature of this process is construed as incidental, untrue, or in some way "not subject to conscious deliberation and reflection" (as in accounts using a linear-analytic framework), then society may approve of "various forms of intervention into individual decision making," such as "the medicalization of all sorts of human behavior"[38] from homosexuality to crime. Hence, those with a commitment to advancing human potential and to feminist principles (such as "the valorization of subjective experience"[39]) should choose explanatory frameworks with prior knowledge of how a framework tends to construe "relevance and interpretation of data"[40]: what sort of constraints does a framework place on human potential from the outset?

Longino claims that "knowledge is shaped by the assumptions, values, and interests of a culture, and that, within limits, one can choose one's culture";[41] as a result, scientists are responsible for deciding how they will perform "establishment science" as well as perform socially and politically accountable science.[42] Scientists, consequently, should ask questions about the brain and about sex-related behaviors through frameworks that "emphasize the enabling rather than the limiting aspects of biology."[43] Longino notes that a post-Enlightenment, highly secular society such as ours entertains the claims of science quite seriously; "social relations and cultural frameworks"[44] inform scientific practice as contextual values, but scientific practice reciprocally influences the dynamics of social relations and cultural frameworks, including our formal channels of political access (i.e., voting)[45] and informal social policies.[46] For example, scientists will continue to produce "biologically determinist theories" that will, in turn, foster a dimorphic (social) classification of gender that will, in turn, influence our (social) ideals of personhood.[47] If this mutual influence between science and socio-political contexts is inevitable in our culture, then scientists have an obligation to foster positive (potential) conceptions of human capacity through carefully constructing their theories and interpreting data.

Lambert's Perspective and its Difficulties

Lambert differs in her appraisal of the two models juxtaposed in Longino's discussion. Lambert identifies similar problems with the socio-political implications of linear-analytic frameworks, as in evolutionary and hormonal/genetic studies, that purport to demonstrate that biological differences are "universally necessary"[48] and "inevitable."[49] She points out the ways in which the findings of such studies "have frequently been generalized by analogy to 'explain' observed sex differences in human behavior."[50] While Longino points out that the linear-analytic and dynamic interactive models both possess comparably strong data and correlational weaknesses, Lambert appears to suggest strongly that models which do not allow for at least a very weak interactionism may be constitutively flawed. Lambert criticizes any model that does not permit weak interaction, at the very least: "To equate biological with intrinsic, inflexible, or preprogrammed is an unfortunate misuse of the term biological."[51] Therefore, biological accounts that employ a strict conception of the linear-analytic model in which biochemical events are schematized into a fixed, unidirectional sequence fail to recognize that "[b]ehavior is itself a biological phenomenon, an interaction between organism and environment."[52] Models which do not account for environmental variables are mistakenly assuming that "an intrinsically induced deviation from some hypothetical, 'normal' course of development" could occur that ordinarily would not occur "in the total absence of extrinsic influences." But, as Lambert indicates, such a total absence "would be the abnormal situation" since systems are not "pre-wired" in such a fashion.[53]

Because Lambert does not approve of any model that does not recognize the interactive nature of biological development and an organism's environment (specifically, biology's dependence on the stimulation provided by environmental factors for organizational clues),[54] she is skeptical of science's ability to locate the point of "precise separation of the biological bases into those which are intrinsic in origin and those which are not."[55] Like Longino, Lambert recognizes the mutual influencing of science and society, yet Lambert's response assumes a different character than Longino's because she does not believe in the constitutive integrity of strong linear-analytic explanatory frameworks.

Lambert frames the problematic: she locates the possibility of egalitarian social reform measures as a function of the ways in which society generally construes social inequality. Briefly described, people are more likely to make sacrifices and/or commit to progressive measures if a group/individual is disenfranchised as a result of the social system's failure than if the group/individual simply did not fare well through "nature's lottery."[56] Thus, the success of the possible implementation of more egalitarian policies depends on science's ability to tell us "if an observed difference is due to biology or society."[57]

However, on Lambert's account, science cannot, unfortunately, provide such a "quantitative answer, a 'biological limit' of socialization."[58] What should we do? According to Lambert, science need not be considered a member of this debate, for it cannot give us that answer which these debates require: how much of social inequality due to sex-differentiated behaviors is biological, and how much of the biological is really environmental. This question around which the debate is located is not "answerable" in scientific terms; put bluntly, naively maintaining the role of science in the question's determination is "strategically unwise" since the resultant arguing serves to "delay social reform."[59] As if this response did not serve to remove science securely from the social policy debate, Lambert also mentions that "[o]ur operating criteria for redress or recompense of differences (or their social consequences) are usually severity of need and cost of remedy — not the cause of the difference."[60]

Like Longino, Lambert recognizes that science has become the arbiter of critical debates about human nature and consequent moral obligations; as Longino says, "[T]he sciences, buttressed by their contemporary spectacular practical successes, have come to fill the void left by religion."[61] Longino addresses the role that the sciences tend to play in our culture, even if critics can point to the sciences' fallibility and limitations. Although Lambert perceives linear-analytic models to be constitutively negligible as well as politically pernicious, she performs an impractical and counter-intuitive move: she seeks to dispose science from its unwitting throne. Lambert simply insists that science cannot play such a role in debates about social policy and about what human nature *really* is.

Conclusion

Lambert's account is weak in comparison to Longino's. First, her attitude does not address the problem that in our cultural framework, whether justified or not, individuals *do* look to science as a means of knowing. Next, if Lambert can recognize the way in which a highly controversial and politically charged debate has been framed around the potential theories proffered by scientists, one would expect her to urge scientists to bear in mind the inevitably ideological character of their work; instead, she implores those seeking answers to concentrate on practical measures to achieve greater social equality in ways which are compatible even with presently observed sex differences, and focusing, not on their causation, but on their possible relevance to specific social function.[62]

Third, this passage, as well as her point mentioned above regarding recompense as determined by need and not by cause, manifests her strangely narrow view: it appears that she does not anticipate or speak to the problem underlying these admittedly time-consuming arguments — the probable circular nature of the debate itself. For example, it seems that if we took Lambert's advice to devise "practical measures," we would at some point probably ask the same questions that drove us to the present aporia: how can we be certain that the direction which we choose is justified as we invent these practical measures? Shouldn't we know whether to focus our energies on more "nature" issues instead of "nurture" ones, or vice versa? How did such need and social inequality happen in our society in the first place? If we know this answer, then perhaps we can prevent it before it occurs. We have traveled full circle to the starting point. Finally, it is not clear that Lambert's particular conception of biological processes and behavior is "correct" for all fields of research or for every research program within a particular field; she has not reviewed enough evidence or contexts to make her claims conclusive regarding the allegedly universal nature of behavior and biology.[63] Longino, in contrast, does not exclude from the outset a model that may be functional for some research (or for aspects of it) as long as it speaks adequately to the constitutive demands of the relevant community; she also recognizes the value of a plurality of models and theories that may act as tools of analysis or as optional viewpoints.

Longino and Lambert both identify how "the ubiquity of [sex-related] assumptions ... preclude [scientific studies'] ideological or value-related character,"[64] as Longino described in detail through her accounts of the linear hormonal and selectionist theories. Yet they frame their interpretation of that problem and their prescriptive responses on different understandings of the interaction between science and the social sphere and of scientists' moral responsibilities. With history and case studies to support her beliefs, Longino accepts that the outcome/implications of scientific research are both a cause and an effect of societal processes (of which they are already a part); as a result, she maintains that scientists must labor to articulate their implicit assumptions and to scrutinize the explicit ones with knowledge of the critical intersection of science and society. With history and case studies to support her beliefs, Lambert accepts that science is a limited mode of revealing human nature and of guiding social progress, and thereby proceeds to remove it as a means of determining social policy. Longino perceives the dynamic interaction and mutual influencing that occur among all parts, including the sciences, in the social whole; scientists must attend to predicating their theories and data interpretation on socially responsible notions of human equality, decision-making capacities, and rights to self-determination since science will influence cultural norms and mores whether that influence is logically valid and morally justified or not. Lambert refuses to recognize the latter half of Longino's pragmatic perceptions; hence, she does not direct feminists or scientists toward a feasible goal that could possibly benefit both science and social equality as does Longino.

NOTES

1. Helen E. Longino, *Science as Social Knowledge: Values and Objectivity in Scientific Inquiry* (Princeton: Princeton University Press, 1990).

2. Helen H. Lambert, "Biology and Equality: A Perspective on Sex Differences," *Sex and Scientific Inquiry*. Harding, Sandra, and Jean O'Barr (editors). Chicago: University of Chicago Press, 1987: 125-145.

3. Longino 133-161. This chapter elucidates the constitutive aspects of the two respective research projects, not their social and political impact.

4. The constitutive aspects of these research projects are related to the "constitutive values" of science which "are the source of rules determining what constitutes acceptable scientific practice or scientific method" (*Ibid.* 4) within a particular field. The constitutive values of scientific practice posit what is "good" and "bad" science; for example, "reliance upon an explanatory model or set of background assumptions does not demonstrate bad methodology" since data is never free "of some background assumptions" (*Ibid.* 162).

5. The contextual values of science refer to those "personal, social, and cultural ... preferences about what ought to be" the determining rules of science; as a result, "they belong to the social and cultural environment in which science is done" (*Ibid.* 4).

6. Any "explanatory framework," on Longino's account, delineates the type of entities that enter into a normative description of a phenomenon and their relations to the phenomenon; it also describes the relations among the entities themselves, and what makes them particularly relevant. Explanatory frameworks rarely make the ideological character of their scientific programs explicit (*Ibid.* 134).

7. *Ibid.* 138.

8. *Ibid.* 189.

9. *Ibid.* 139.

10. *Ibid.*

11. *Ibid.*

12. *Ibid.* 157.

13. *Ibid.*

14. *Ibid.*

15. *Ibid.* 155.

16. *Ibid.* 144-145.

17. *Ibid.* 145.

18. *Ibid.*

19. *Ibid.*

20. *Ibid.* 148.

21. For a simplified, schematic description of phasic reentry, see pp. 146-147 (Longino). For a more complete summary of the development of primary and secondary repertoires, see pp. 144-146 (Longino). Repetition of the specific events involved in these processes is more distracting than helpful to my main point here.

22. *Ibid.* 147.

23. *Ibid.* 175.

24. *Ibid.* 189.

25. *Ibid.* 158.

26. *Ibid.*

27. *Ibid.* 159.

28. Lambert does indicate the exception with two studies on Eskimos (*Ibid.* 140).

29. Longino 160-161.

30. *Ibid.* 161.

31. *Ibid.* 138.

32. *Ibid.* 167.
33. *Ibid.* 164-175. These are Longino's three categorizations.
34. *Ibid.* 77. Specifically, refer to her four criteria for objectivity for greater detail.
35. *Ibid.* 154.
36. *Ibid.* 158.
37. *Ibid.* 166.
38. *Ibid.* 174.
39. *Ibid.* 190.
40. *Ibid.* 189.
41. *Ibid.* 191.
42. *Ibid.*
43. *Ibid.* 175-176.
44. *Ibid.* 176.
45. *Ibid.* 165.
46. Informal policies are "institutional practices or policies of action that are generally accepted but not legally or administratively articulated or prescribed." They are rooted in "social value"" (*Ibid.* 164).
47. *Ibid.* 171. Longino defines "ideals of personhood" as "models to which we aspire or whose realization is urged upon us" (*Ibid.* 167). The dilemma is that an ideal and a stereotype may possess the same content, but a "stereotype has a descriptive function, and an ideal has a prescriptive function." Thus, persons who do not conform to ideals may be victimized or derided since its counterpart in a stereotype indicates what is "true" of, for example, all men and masculinity and all women and femininity. (*Ibid.* 168)
48. Lambert 125.
49. *Ibid.* 126.
50. *Ibid.* 127.

51. *Ibid.* 132.

52. *Ibid.*

53. *Ibid.*

54. "It seems likely that complex, multiple causation is the rule. ... Social environment multiplies and magnifies, in many ways, an average kernel of intrinsic predisposition" (*Ibid.* 141).

55. *Ibid.* 133.

56. *Ibid.* 143.

57. *Ibid.* 142.

58. *Ibid.*

59. *Ibid.* 144.

60. *Ibid.*

61. Longino 164.

62. *Ibid.* 145.

63. *Ibid.* 132-133 (especially).

64. Longino 133.

REFERENCES

Barnes, Barry and David Bloor. "Relativism, Rationalism and the Sociology of Knowledge." *Rationality and Relativism.* Martin Hollis and Steven Lukes (editors). Cambridge: MIT Press, 1982. 21-47.

Biology and Gender Study Group. "The Importance of Feminist Critique for Contemporary Cell Biology." *Feminism and Science.* Nancy Tuana (editor). Indiana: Indiana University Press, 1989. 172-187.

Collins, Patricia Hill. "Learning From the Outsider Within: The Sociological Significance of Black Feminist Thought." *Beyond Methodology.* Mary Fonow and Judith Cook (editors). Indiana: Indiana University Press, 1991. 35-59.

Haraway, Donna. *Simians, Cyborgs and Women.* New York: Routledge Press, 1991.

Harding, Sandra. *Whose Science, Whose Knowledge?* Cornell: Cornell University Press, 1990.

Hempel, Carl Gustav. *Philosophy of Natural Science.* Englewood Cliffs: Prentice Hall, 1966.

Keller, Evelyn Fox. *Reflections on Gender and Science.* Yale: Yale University Press, 1985.

Kuhn, Thomas. *The Structure of Scientific Revolutions.* 2nd. ed. Chicago: University of Chicago Press, 1970.

Lambert, Helen H. "Biology and Equality: A Perspective on Sex Differences." *Sex and Scientific Inquiry.* Sandra Harding and Jean O'Barr (editors). Chicago: University of Chicago Press, 1987. 125-145.

Longino, Helen E. *Science as Social Knowledge: Values and Objectivity in Scientific Inquiry.* Princeton: Princeton University Press, 1990.

Rosser, Sue V. "Feminist Scholarship in the Sciences: Where Are We Now and When Can We Expect a Theoretical Breakthrough?" *Feminism and Science.* Nancy Tuana (editor). Indiana: Indiana University Press, 1989. 3-14.

Subjective versus Objective Reality: An Examination Through Physics and Philosophy

Michael Joseph
SUNY - Oneonta

In Metaphysics, there are two very different ways of thinking about perception and reality. It is important to distinguish between the two because the view that is held, either subjective or objective, influences not only how you view reality, but also how you view yourself in relation to the rest of reality.

The objective account of perception is based on the premise that one can actually escape reality in order to perceive it from a detached perspective. It assumes that you can understand reality, not as one of its parts, but as an outsider looking in with detached, impartial objectivity.

The subjective account of perception, on the other hand, argues that to understand reality you must also understand the affect you have on reality. In other words you must view yourself as a part of the greater whole and understand that your very presence can alter reality.

An example of the debate between these two views can be seen through the old riddle: *If a tree falls in a forest when there is no one around to hear it, does it make a noise?* In other words: if there is no one to observe reality, does it really happen?

There is a revolutionary debate occurring today between the scientists that examine the macroscopic world known as classical physics and a new school of thought which is known as the new physics. The new physics is based on observations of subatomic particles, including quantum mechanics and relativity theory. Classical theory believes that the world can be observed objectively and the new physics gives strong support to a new theory that reality is really subjective. This paper will examine the metaphysical implications of the debate.

Plato tried to answer this debate through his theory of forms. Although it may be a controversial interpretation, I believe that Plato sided with the objective view. I believe he thought that the world could be understood as an object. He believed in a separation of the physical and the mental realms. Plato placed thought on a higher level than sensation. He believed that through thought we can understand what our senses alone cannot. This ability of thought was supposedly a type of gift to the mortals from the Gods. Plato believed that man once lived among the Gods and had knowledge of Divine affairs. He believed that we once knew and understood the ideal of perfection through forms. Plato also believed that our memory gets clouded because of our reincarnation to earth; but we still have the memory of perfection. Through this memory we are able to understand the forms or things in themselves, as the following example shows:

> Is there such a thing as fire in itself, and do all these other realities of which we use this phrase so and so in itself exist? Or are the things we see and perceive by our other senses the only true realities? ... If intelligence and true opinion are different in kind, then these things in themselves certainly exist, forms imperceptible to our senses, but apprehended by thought.[1]

Through this example we can see that Plato believed in forms in themselves. In other words, things exist independently of us: the subject. This is an objective view of the world because we can understand reality without becoming a part of it. Through the mind Plato believed we can understand everything from its original form. There is a type of perfection in each object and we can understand the physical reality through these mental ideas or forms.

It is important to note the paradox that is implicit in these claims. It may be thought by some that Plato advocated a subjective view of reality because we see it through forms which are found in the human mind. It is important to point out that this is incorrect because he believed that the human mind did not create these forms, but merely remembered them from when men lived among Gods. Plato spends a great deal of time in the *Timaeus* explaining how the Gods created everything. Therefore Plato can be seen as advocating an objective view of reality because the Gods created these forms, and man can understand them. This means that the human mind is not responsible for creating the reality that it is interpreting; therefore Plato sides with the objective view.

The objective view of reality was the prevalent view held by many scientists for many generations. They believed that they could conduct experiments to understand the nature of the universe. They believed that they could observe nature and understand reality. What they did not understand is that they can not escape reality; they are a part of it. One example which began to change this way of thinking is the fact that light can behave as either a particle or a wave. This puzzled scientists till Bohr came to the realization that the nature of the light and our observations of it were relative to what we did. In other words the nature of light is subjective:

> An independent reality in the ordinary physical sense can be ascribed neither to the phenomena nor to the agencies of observation.[2]

This quote from Bohr has incredible philosophical implications. It proposes that things do not exist independently; they exist as a reaction to something. This is clearly subjective, since the subject determines the reaction and thus the reality that actually occurs. In reference to Plato, this theory assumes that the forms do not exist independently of the human mind, but in response to the human mind. In fact forms are a creation of the human mind as a result of a reaction with reality.

The struggle to understand the nature of the reality of the light particle, and why it behaves as it does has ended in futility. The Copenhagen Interpretation of Quantum Mechanics said basically that the attempt to understand the nature of an independently existing quantum mechanical reality is unnecessary. We only need to understand the result, not the cause. This created a great amount of debate between classical physics which viewed the world objectively and quantum mechanics which views phenomenon in a subjective way. Classical physics approached reality with the view that either something either exists, or it does not. The new physics, on the other hand, views things as having a possibility to exist. There is a clear tension here. This was demonstrated with light in a famous double slit experiment.

There are two slits in a board when a single photon of light is fired. If one slit is open the photon acts like a particle. If both slits are open the light acts like a wave. Classical physics would say that it is either a wave or a particle. Since we can not observe this directly till after it happens, quantum mechanics speaks in probabilities of something becoming a reality. In other words there is a probability before the photon is fired that it will be a wave, and another probability that it will be a photon. Since the reality that will happen depends on what the observers do — open one slit or two — we in effect are creating reality or the potential for reality. This is subjective since the subject (us) determines or at least affects the outcome of the reality of the experiment. This was a revolutionary discovery in physics. If we create reality, then we are a part of it and it would not exist without us.

In the subatomic realm direct observation is impossible. This is not because we do not have the tools but because it is impossible to know, with precision, both the position and the momentum of a subatomic particle. This is known as Heisenberg's uncertainty principle. We can only know one of these attributes at a given time. The more we know about one attribute, the less we know about the other. This is a direct contradiction to Newtonian Physics (Classical) which believes that we can know both. Although we cannot know the exact properties in quantum mechanics we can know the probabilities. This is the probability of something occurring or something in fact becoming reality. In other words:

> Quantum physics abandons the laws which govern individual events and states directly the statistical laws which govern collections of events. Quantum mechanics can tell us how a group of particles will behave, but the only thing it can say about an individual particle is how it probably will behave.[3]

This deals with the ability to predict what will happen by using a probability. This is controversial because if there is a possibility of something becoming a reality then there is no fixed reality. The reality is completely subjective, because a particle does not actualize or become reality until we can observe what happened. According to this theory, nothing exists until we know that it exists. Although I think they go a little too far, it is necessary to explore this possibility in order to understand it. This is well in the subjective realm of understanding reality. This theory (Copenhagen) states that until we know what happened only a possibility of it happening exists.

Therefore reality is completely based on the subject because it claims that reality cannot exist on its own. In other words, a tree does not fall in the forest unless there is someone there to hear it and that person actually hears it.

Another way of interpreting puzzling quantum mechanical results is called *the many worlds theory*. This theory states that in the subatomic realm there not only are there many possible outcomes, but they all occur, at the same time in parallel universes.

> All of the mutually exclusive possibilities contained ... of an observed system that (according to the Copenhagen Interpretation) do not actualize ... actually do actualize, but not in this branch of the universe.[4]

This theory is also subjective because the version of reality that actualizes or becomes real depends on which world the subject happens to be in. In a different frame of reality the exact opposite result of what happened in one reality occurs in yet another reality. Every possible result that can occur in fact becomes reality in a different world. Since the world in which the subject is present determines the reality that they observe, reality is again dependent on the subject, therefore subjective.

The analogy of Schrödinger's cat gives a better understanding of these different views of the same phenomena. Consider the following scenario:

> A cat is placed inside a box. Inside the box is a device which can release a gas, instantly killing the cat. A random event determines whether the gas is released or not. There is no way of knowing, outside of looking into the box, what happens inside it. The box is sealed and the experiment is activated. A moment later the gas has either been released or has not been released. The question is without looking, what has happened inside the box.[5]

This is a good analogy to help understand the behavior of subatomic particles as well as the way in which the classic view contradicts the theories of the new physics. The view of classical physics would be that either the cat is dead or it is not. Either way the result would happen regardless of our actions. This is clearly objective. The Copenhagen interpretation described earlier would say that the cat is in a type of limbo. This limbo contains the possibilities that either the cat is alive or the cat is not alive. When we open the box, one of these two possible realities actualizes and the other vanishes. Therefore reality does not actually become reality until the subject realizes it. The many worlds theory would say that both realities actualize. In one world the cat is alive and in a parallel world the cat is not alive. The reality that is experienced by the subject depends on the world in which the subject finds himself. This shows the conflict between the classical physics and the revolutionary thought of the new physics.

The classical theory of objectivity is also being destroyed through Einstein's Theory of Relativity. Einstein's first rebuttal of classical physics is based on the constancy of the speed of light. He turned a counterintuitive observation into a postulate:

> ... whenever we make a measurement of the velocity of light, regardless of whether we are in motion or at rest relative to the light source, we always get the same result.[6]

According to Classical physics this makes no sense, if we are moving relative to the source of light, the velocity of light should be affected; but it is not. This is an important element of Einstein's Special Theory of Relativity. Although this contradicted classical objective physics, Einstein knew that you could not disagree with the experimental results. The only answer was to assume that the motion of the measurement devices

> ... change from one frame of reference to the other in just such a way that the speed of light always appears to be the same... The speed of light appears constant because the rods and clocks used to measure it vary from one frame of reference to another depending on their motion.[7]

Einstein proposed that the measurements remained constant because the instruments themselves change. The rods would actually get shorter as its velocity increased and clocks actually slow their rhythm as their velocity increases thereby measuring the speed of light as a constant. These observations are only possible to an observer at rest, not the holder of the clocks and rods. There is a distinction made between proper time and relative time.

> Proper lengths and proper times always appear normal. What we see if we are stationary and observe a rod and a clock traveling very fast relative to us is the relative length of the moving rod and the relative time of the moving clock. The relative length is always shorter than the proper length and the relative time is always slower than the proper time.[8]

This theory clearly states that reality is based on the motion of what is being observed and the motion of the observer itself. The implications of this theory are immense. The classical theory was shown to be invalid at the microscopic (subatomic) level of the world through the results obtained by the new physics. However, the new physics did not prove that the macroscopic world could not be observed objectively. The objective classical idea of a reality that exists in and of itself assumes that only one possible reality exists. This theory of relativity proposes that space and time are relative or subjective to motion; therefore since we exist in space and we can only observe things in space and time, there is no possible way to observe things objectively.

Perhaps an example will help make my point more clear. It was once thought that we could not possibly affect the planetary motion, therefore it must be possible to observe it objectively. Now we can see that our observations are dependent not only on the motion of our planet, but the possible motion of the universe and space and time itself. Now that the very foundations of our reality are relative, how can the objective classical view of reality hold? It can not. The very nature of our cognitive ability to understand reality is being challenged. The belief that we can step outside reality and observe phenomena objectively has been seriously questioned by the new physics in the area of quantum mechanics and relativity theory. The reality which we perceive is perceived according to our standards of sense perception and is often subject to our own creation. Since all that can be understood, can be understood only through the human mind, which can alter and even create reality (as the new physics shows), reality itself must be subjective.

NOTES

1. Plato, p. 71.
2. Zukav, p. 95.
3. Zukav, p. 35
4. Zukav, p. 84.
5. Zukav, p. 85.
6. Zukav, p. 135.
7. Zukav, p. 138.
8. Zukav, p. 139.

REFERENCES

Plato. *Timaeus and Critias*. New York: Penguin Books, 1971.

Zukav, Gary. *The Dancing Wu Li Masters*. New York: Bantam Books, 1979.

Exploring the Universe, From Plato to Einstein and Beyond

Alex Slater
SUNY - Oneonta

If we want to explore the universe, the first thing we need is a mode of transportation. Last time I checked, NASA was not renting any of their vehicles out, so the spaceship idea doesn't work. Which is just as well. Plato and his cohorts had no need for such things; so why do we? Plato and anyone else before 1960 AD had only to use their imagination to traverse the universe. (Why not? Eastern Mystics have been doing this for centuries.)

Now we have our mode of transport: the mind. The next thing we need to do is prepare the craft for its trip. This involves getting your mind into the right state of mind (???). To put it in a less paradoxical way: you have to think of this from the right perspective or, if you prefer, from the right point of reference.

Our trip is going to start as a trip through time. Way back to Ancient Greece in the time of the great philosopher Plato. In order to join Plato on his quest for reality and his explorations of the universe we have to put ourselves into his frame of reference. Okay, how do we do that? We read things that he wrote (e.g. *Timaeus* and *Critias*) and use our imagination.

(You do have an imagination don't you? If not then go find one because that is your passport to the universe and the only way to join in on this trip.)

Journal Entry 1
The World of Plato (365 BC)

Ancient Greece, the birthplace of western philosophy. The pre-Socratics gave rise to the ideas that the universe was made up of specific things. What specific things? It depends on who you talk to. Some believed that everything was fire (Heraclitus). Gorgias thought that all was "nothing." Out of all this seeming confusion comes Socrates. Socrates was an odd one who admitted that he knew nothing. In essence he knew that the universe was much too complicated for him to grasp.

Socrates no doubt schooled Plato in the ideas of the other philosophers and thus helped form his ideas, but how much and in exactly what way is not really known. We can imagine (our passport) Plato standing in the courtyard underneath an olive tree with one of his own students (possibly Aristotle) discussing reality and further forming his ideas. His ideas were just that, "forms."

Plato is talking about how there are four parts of reality: a Divine Creator, Being, Becoming, and the Receptacle of Becoming. Being is the start of everything, the forms or ideas that we have about the universe. These forms are always Becoming. Becoming what? Reality. Where does this all happen? The Receptacle of Becoming. This is confusing. Who or what does all this? The Divine Creator. Okay I really am lost now. Let's go a bit further back in time to see if Socrates can help us.

The World of Socrates (410 BC)

We find Socrates sitting alone and explain to him our dilemma.[1] After thinking about it for a while he tries to relieve our frustration with an example. "You have these forms or ideas called 'Being'," he says. "Ideas can only exist in the mind. They are thus intangible, eternal, and can never be changed. As odd as it sounds these forms are formless. Now this Divine Creator, let's say Zeus, decides to make these forms tangible."

"So Zeus orders the Becoming," I say.

"Exactly," says Socrates. "He orders the formless to become formed according to the form of the forms. All of this becoming takes place in the Receptacle of Being. Think of it this way: there is a King (Divine Creator) who has heard all of his subjects crying for soup. He also hears them yelling out what kinds of soup they would like to have (the abstract forms). Then he orders his servants to make the soup (the tangible ever-changing becoming) in a large pot (the Receptacle of Becoming)."

"Okay, that makes sense. But what is the soup?"

"Reality, of course," says Socrates.

Now that we have the premise for Plato's view on reality, let's pop back in on him and his student to hear what else he has to say.

Back to the World of Plato (365 BC)

We find Plato explaining that the reality we live in was created by a "Demiurge" (a God). This Demiurge used the formless ideas to form the substance of the Universe. Thus, reality was "born." There is one problem though: in the "act of Becoming," the original idea was lost. It was replaced by a paradigm or a shadow. We are tricked into the idea that the reality we see is the original idea of the Universe. This reality is just a shadow of what really is. What really exists are the forms (Being). In the act of Becoming, they become shadows of their former self. Only when we can look beyond the confines of our "senses" can we really see reality in its original form (pure Being).[2]

Plato uses the word *episteme* when describing the truth of Being. He uses the word *doxa* to describe the shadows created by Becoming. This idea is also the basis for the different levels of reality (i.e. the truth and the shadows). All levels of reality are connected to each other. For example, humans are a part of the physical world (the body) and the eternal world (the soul). This means there is a connection between the two. Not only humans, but anything that consists of the eternal idea and the physical body is a connection of the multiple levels of reality.

"Whoa there Plato," I say out of nowhere. "If I have a connection to another level of reality, why don't I have any idea of this so-called Truth?"

"That is an easy question to answer stranger," Plato says rather arrogantly. "The human soul carries *eidola*, or imprints of the forms. We have forgotten the originals and the *eidola* are clouded by the shadows created in the Becoming. Thus, we have a connection; we just don't know how to use it."

"I see," say I. "It is sort of like having a slave to do your bidding, but he does not speak your language. Potentially, you may learn his language or he may learn yours. Until then, there is not much you can do with him."

"It is interesting that you should mention language," Plato replies. "I have some thoughts about rhetoric and dialectic which I would like to share with you."

"I would love to stay and chat, but my friend and I must be on our way. There is so little time and so much to learn."

"Time," I hear Plato call, "belongs only to the realm of Becoming. Being is timeless."

Journal Entry 2
The World of Wu Li (1803 AD)

Thomas Young's "doubt slit experiment" showed that light was wave-like. In this experiment, light passing through two slits in a screen creates an interference pattern. Since only waves create interference patterns, light must be wave-like.

The World of Wu Li (1900 AD)

Max Planck finds that energy is released in Quanta, or packets. These packets have a constant size depending on what color or kind they were. This constant size is called "Planck's Constant." At the time this was considered a major find.[3] But it was not until Einstein published his *Special Theory of Relativity* that Modern Physics was truly born. Relativity Theory and Quantum Mechanics make up the foundations of this new Physics.

Okay, you are asking yourself, "What does this have to do with reality or the universe?" Right? Well, physics is the new western way of explaining the universe. In laying the groundwork of Modern Physics, Einstein and Planck started a new way of seeing the universe/reality that was unthinkable using Newtonian assumptions.

The World of Wu Li (1905 AD)

In 1905, Albert Einstein published three very important papers. One described molecular motion, another was his special theory of relativity, and the third was his discovery of the Particle or Quantum-like nature of light.

"Wait," you may say. "Didn't Young prove that light was wave-like?"

Yes he did.

"So how can something be wave-like and particle like?"

It depends on how you look at it. This seemingly impossible puzzle was just the first of many irrational things that subatomic particles were doing. Perhaps we can find someone to help explain these puzzles.

We discover Albert waiting patiently for his secretary "Marge" to assist him with editing his papers. "OY, I've always been lousy at spelling."

We take advantage of this break in his concentration to ask him what makes light particle-like even though Young proved it was wave-like.

"It goes like this," Albert explains. "A stream of light, let's say from this bulb, goes forward in a beam. The beam is made up of hundreds of thousands of little particles called 'photons'. The photons are like billiard balls. Every time one of these 'balls' hits an electron from a different atom it knocks it away. Very similar to a 'break' in the game of billiards (the photon being the cue ball and the rest of the balls being electrons)."

"Okay, so how does this make light particle-like?"

"My dear friend, if light is made up of photons, which is what the photoelectric effect shows, photons are particles!"

"So, how can light be both a particle and a wave?"

"I can't explain it, I just prove it."

"Let's get this straight. If light is particle-like and wave-like, does this mean that our view of reality is not what it really is?"

"You got it kiddo," answers a voice from behind us.

"Okay, now who are you?" I ask.

"Marge, secretary to everyone. I don't just sit here and look pretty, I know what's going on."

"So, how come the views of reality are so different now than in Plato's time?"

"Honey, they just seem different. Plato said that true reality was not what it seemed. What we see is a shadow; the truth is hidden. When we do see the truth we most likely will not be able to comprehend it (like light being both a wave and a particle). Albert is a very smart man; go ahead ask him about his special theory of relativity."

"Relativity?"

"Just go ask him."

"Okay, Albert, I give. What is this about a special theory of relativity?"

"The truth can only be seen with a child's mind. This means that as you grow, you are indoctrinated with what people perceive to be the truth, but it is not. Everything they witness is clouded by judgments and recollections of other things. Thus they never see things as they really are, but as they want them to be. A child on the other hand has no such experience to draw upon and is not clouded by misconceptions; the child sees the truth. (This is as long as his parents do not censor his learning. When this happens, the child's view of the world is tainted. It usually happens when they start being taught instead of being allowed to learn.) I have taken what everyone has found out about physics and seen them with a child's mind. What I took from everyone has helped me formulate my theory. The theory is about how appearances are relative. Appearances are not necessarily what is real, but they are what is presented to us. Things that are real are 'absolutes'. These absolutes never change. Their appearances change. For example, a man flies by at a constant speed and I am standing still. He is holding a rod. To him, the appearance of the rod measures one length. To me, with the rod flying by, it will measure something else. The actual or absolute length of the rod is still the same, but as something approaches the speed of light it appears, to me (the one standing still), to be smaller. If I could watch it as it sped up, it would actually appear to be shrinking![4] Using my special theory we can transpose each other's results and find a way to agree about the length of the rod. So in essence my theory is not about what is relative but what is invariant. I wonder if Marge would let me change it's name?"

"Okay, I get the idea behind your special theory. I just have one question, why is it special?"

"Ah, you see my theory has one significant drawback. It only works when there is no acceleration for either of the observers. I hope to someday formulate a theory that expands to all types of motion. There has to be some way to transpose information gained during different acceleration rates."

"So you are now looking for a 'General' theory that works everywhere at all speeds."

"Yes, you could say that. But it will probably take the rest of my life. Can you wait?"

"Sure, I'll see you in ten years."

"Ten years?'

The World of Wu Li (1915 AD)

"Let's hear it Einstein my boy, what do you have to say about your new theory of relativity?'

"I am not quite sure who you are, but you do look familiar. Since you ask... You cannot have a complete physical theory unless every element of the physical reality has a counterpart in the physical theory. My new theory has this one-to-one correspondence. The special theory was lacking because it was useful only in 'special' situations. The transposing of the relative information from the coordinate systems was easy using $E=MC^2$. Now when you look at other coordinate systems you can transpose information even if the frameworks are accelerated or subject to different measures of gravity."

"So gravity is the common denominator between coordinate systems?"

"Sort of, but to understand it fully you would need to know advanced mathematics. Do you know calculus or geometry?"

"No. But I get the idea, thanks for your time."

"Just a minute, there is one more thing you need to understand. In addition to the macrocosm, our world of observations, there are at least two more realms: the microcosm and the cosmos. The very small and the very large. I have not yet managed a complete explanation of reality. As it stands there is no way for us to transpose what goes on in each of the three different levels of reality onto each other. Things that make sense in the subatomic world do not make sense here and we are not quite sure what happens in the greater universe. My next goal is to find a unified field equation. Such an equation would unite the three levels about which I have spoken. Reality is a complicated thing, my friend."

The World of Wu Li
(hanging out in the middle of time)

Okay, let's sit here and digest all of this information. At this point in time we have the belief that reality is made up of at least three different levels. The macrocosm that we live in, the microcosm that we cannot see, and the cosmos that is too big to comprehend. Newtonian physics attempts to explain what is going on here in the macrocosm. Quantum mechanics attempts to explain the microcosm. Astronomy and Einsteinian principles attempt to explain the cosmos.

The problem with Newtonian physics is that it does not work well in conjunction with quantum mechanics. Also any attempt to explain the greater universe is largely speculation. According to Einstein a true unified field equation would cross over and explain them all. Plato's view of reality was so much simpler.

While prepping for this leg of the trip, I read a condensed version of the new view on reality (*The Dancing Wu Li Masters*, by Gary Zukav). This book explains subatomic phenomenon better than I ever could. The next leg of this journey goes beyond this book and it's view on reality. It explores my own thought (scary thought, eh?). Part of this leg concerns problems I have with the new physics. The rest deals with my own view of reality as influenced by my own personal Becoming.

Journal Entry 3
The World of Me (1996 AD)

In my opinion the biggest problem with the quantum theory is the whole idea of probability waves. Schrödinger was one "out there" kind of guy. For him to say that his cat was a probability wave until we look at it is, to me, unfeasible. You just don't know whether it was dead or alive. He and many others say the same thing about electrons swirling around the nucleus. "They have a probability of being one place or another". Hogwash!!! They are there; we are just not sure where.

Imagine a baseball with a grain of sand revolving around it. (Officially the sand-grain would be about a hundred yards away from the baseball, but please bear with me.) The grain of sand spins at a certain observable rate. Now just shrink that ball and grain of sand down to the size of the atom. The sand is still revolving at the same "relative" speed, but the size is so much smaller that the apparent spin of the sand is incredibly fast.

Now when we try to observe this sand when it is in atomic size, we need to essentially take a picture of it (using a photographic plate to observe an electron). The only catch is that wherever we take the picture, the sand (electron) is always there. Well, just remember, this sand (electron) is moving super fast. It is essentially moving faster than the camera can take the picture. So no matter where you take the picture it is always there. It actually is always moving, but in taking the picture we have frozen it in time. Nothing collapses. When we take a picture of ourselves, we do not cease to exist anymore. The sand (electron) is still going along its merry way.

Another example of this is to liken an electron to a pendulum swinging in a dark room. Someone then comes in with a flash camera and takes a picture. The picture (Polaroid) is taken into a lighted room and allowed to develop. It develops and we see the pendulum at one point in time. To say that this is the way it is, is to misrepresent reality. The pendulum is always moving and always will be, we just see it at one point in time. The picture is actually a paradigm of reality. It may represent it, but in the end it is not reality.

The World of Me (continued)

That is the main problem that I have with Quantum mechanics. Another one is that they say there is nowhere in the universe that there is absolute non-motion. Again, I say Hogwash!!! If the universe is expanding, then there has to be a center somewhere. At the center is absolute non-motion. The problem that everyone is looking for the center of the universe as if it were a point in space. It is not. The exact center is a point in time. Let me explain. Imagine a telescope powerful enough to look from one end of the universe to the other. At the edge of the universe, at the other side, what do we see? The back of our own heads.

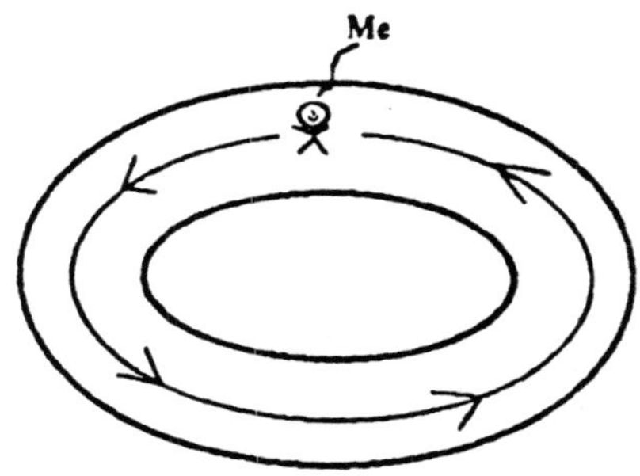

This is not a new theory, it is a form of the "donut" theory. The universe is a never-ending circle. With this image in mind, let's think about a way to get from one side to the other, i.e. the wormhole. The wormhole I have in mind is the microscopic realm. If you are in the microscopic realm (seeing it from its own point of reference) then it appears to you to be the entire cosmos. Ultimately, you are in the cosmos now, on the other side of the universe.

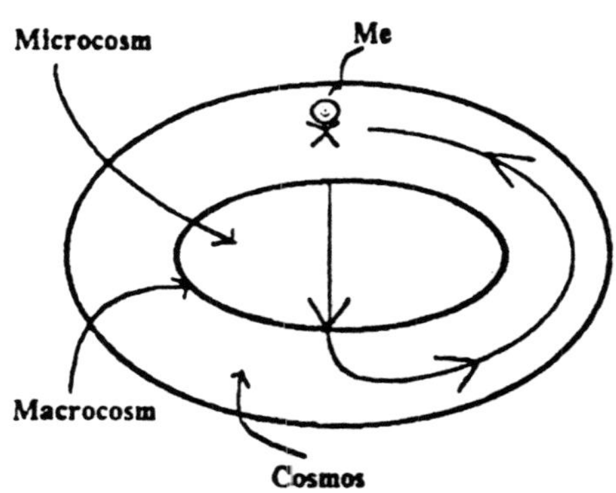

Our macroscopic world is just a thin line between the microscopic and the cosmic levels. Once you slip through this wormhole, the distance around is now cut in half.

Now to get back to the idea of the exact center. The exact moment in time where the microscopic becomes the cosmic is the center. The universe is expanding from a point in time, not a point in space. At that *time* is absolute non-motion. Now that I think about it, this means that there is no microscopic world. It is only our way of seeing the other side of the universe. When we view it, it is microscopic. When we are there it is the cosmos.[5]

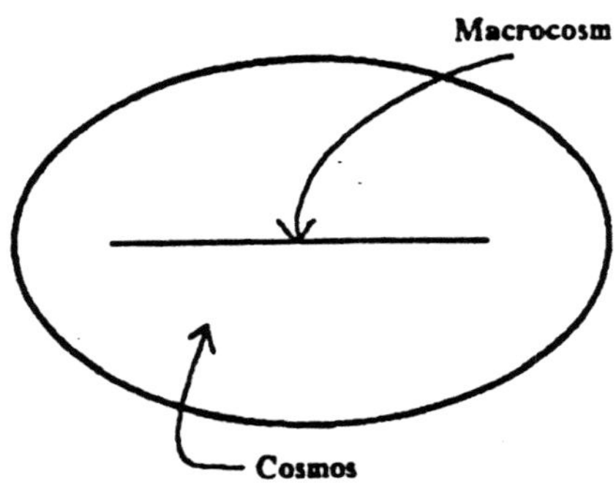

Our travel through time is done. The only difference in the way Plato, Einstein, and I view reality is a matter of perspective. Our views are relative to where we are. It saddens me to think that Einstein died before he could find a unified field equation. Maybe some new, bold, and childlike physicist will find it. I just know that it won't be me. I can't even understand algebra, let alone the quantum math needed for that. My imagination has run out of gas, so if you like you can continue without me, but this is where I get off.

* * *

The fool on the hill, sees the sun going round. The eyes in his head see the world spinning round.

The Fool On The Hill, The Beatles

(Only fools see the world through the Becoming and not the Being.)

* * *

I am he and you are me and we are he and we are all together.

I Am The Eggman, The Beatles

(Cosmic consciousness and interconnectedness.)

NOTES

1. Where did we learn to speak ancient Greek? We didn't; this is imaginary so everyone speaks English.
2. It is interesting to think about Plato's "Allegory of the Cave" (Book VII of *The Republic*) in this way.
3. I guess you have to be a physicist.
4. In effect, this means that the man carrying the rod would appear to be shrinking also and if they exceeded the speed of light then they would become inverted. ***EEEW GROSS!!***
5. If this makes any sense to you, please explain it to me.

REFERENCES

Plato. *The Republic*. New York: Penguin Books, 1955.

Plato. *Timaeus* and *Critias*. New York: Penguin Books, 1971.

Zukav, Gary. *The Dancing Wu Li Masters*. New York: Bantam Books, 1979.

Observing, Observability, and the Importance of a Smiler: A Partial Defense of Strawsonian Events[1]

David Miguel Gray
Columbia University

> "All right," said the Cat; and this time it vanished quite slowly, beginning with the end of the tail, and ending with the grin, which remained some time after the rest had gone.
>
> "Well! I've often seen a cat without a grin," thought Alice; "but a grin without a cat! It's the most curious thing I ever saw in all my life!"
>
> *Alice's Adventures in Wonderland*

We can have butter without buttering anything, but problems arise when we attempt a buttering without butter. Intuitions such as these have created widespread sympathy with the view that while events are dependent upon objects, the opposite is open to debate. Though questions concerning priority and dependency between objects and events have been on the table for some time, little agreement has been reached. Such debate is commonplace since one may find something to disagree with at almost every turn of the issue: the weakness or strength of ontological dependencies, the existence of basic particulars, and the types of dependencies that may exist between objects and events, to name a few.[2] I will attempt to draw some conclusions concerning the symmetrical and asymmetrical dependencies to which objects and events subject each other. I will first discuss what I call "weak dependencies", or "weak priorities" depending on the context, and the reason why I believe these are of little interest to the philosophical community. From here

I will commence a discussion of basic particulars which closely follows Strawson's work in Chapter One of *Individuals*. I will then consider Moravcsik's criticism of Strawson's conception of basic particulars and follow this by my critique of both positions. My critique, primarily of Moravcsik, will rest upon a subtle distinction that both Strawson and Moravcsik fail to draw. Finally, this distinction will lead us into a discussion of two issues: the "strong" dependencies that objects have over events and events over objects, and the symmetrical and asymmetrical relations which hold between them.

Weak Dependency

It is necessary, first and foremost, to construct a framework in which we may consider issues of dependency and priority between events and objects.[3] This will lead us into a non-chronological history of the issue starting with "foundational" dependencies and building up from there. In "Events, Ontology, and Grammar," P. M. S. Hacker poses the basic question: "Are objects ontologically prior to events, or are events ontologically prior to objects, or are both categories equally 'basic' or 'primitive'?" (479). The first type of dependence I would like to discuss is what I call *weak* ontological dependence.[4] This discussion is best started by posing two questions. First, do objects presuppose the existence of events?[5] To grant Hacker's position, we can't imagine objects without the succession of time, and therefore without events.[6] Furthermore, objects are locatable by where they are at certain times and it would be difficult to imagine objects not occupying a certain time, or amount of time. Objects, in this weak sense, depend on events. Second, do events presuppose the existence of objects? Every notion of an event presupposes that it happens at some time. When something happens at some time, according to Hacker, this time is distinguishable from other times through change.

This change is observable in material objects. Moreover, events are locatable by where they are in space, and it would be difficult to imagine events not occupying space, however gerrymandered that space may be. We now see that this weak ontological priority is symmetrical: objects are ontologically dependent on events and events are ontologically dependent on objects.

While this notion of weak ontological priority is a necessary building block for more subtle notions of priority and dependence, I will argue that it is, nevertheless, not an interesting one. Both the conclusions drawn from the preceding examples are fairly obvious and I suspect that few would disagree on this point, with the possible exception of Quineans who wouldn't ask such questions since they consider objects and events to be the same thing. Another type of weak dependence, which I will call *historically-regressive* dependence, deals primarily with the fact that our observations of the world require the existence of an observer.[7] When considering questions of priorities and dependencies, these foundational concepts of observation and the observing/observer relation are fairly clear and not of great philosophical interest. This historically-regressive dependency may also apply to objects that are being observed. This is a weak dependency, as will be explained in detail, because things like a cow's parents, if the cow is the object of observation, are not important to the observation at hand. The main point of historically-regressive dependency is that it brings in events and objects that are not part of the description of an event or object at the present time. A far more interesting philosophical question can be raised by considering an event, i.e. an event with a capital 'E', and the objects involved, or an object and the events involved if you please, and asking if either the object or the event is a basic particular necessary for the existence of the other? By granting these symmetrical, weak ontological dependencies as foundational,[8] and looking towards stronger, and yet more subtle, dependencies to define basic particulars, we up the stakes significantly. The job of the next section will be to address this question.

The Basics: Strawson's Basic Particulars and Asymmetrical Dependencies

In Part Three, Chapter One of *Individuals*, Strawson suggests the need to define the framework that we use in our identification of particulars in common discourse:

> We can make it clear to each other what or which particular things our discourse is about because we can fit together each other's reports and stories into a single picture of the world; and the framework of that picture is a unitary spatio-temporal framework, of one temporal and three spatial dimensions.[9] Hence, as things are, particular-identification in general rests ultimately on the possibility of locating the particular things we speak of in a single unified spatiotemporal system. (38)

This need to define the framework leads Strawson to posing the following questions:

> First, is there a class or category of particulars such that, as things are, it would not be possible to make all the identifying references which we do make to particulars of other classes, unless we made identifying references to particulars of that class, whereas it would be possible to make all the identifying references we do make to particulars of that class without making identifying reference to particulars of the other classes? Second, can we argue to an affirmative answer to this question from the general character of the conceptual scheme I have described? (38-39)

We see here that Strawson explicitly foreshadows the asymmetrical dependence he plans to uncover. Strawson answers the second question first in order to create specific arguments to answer the first question. The type of basic particulars that are to constitute this framework[10] must be those "which can confer upon it its own fundamental characteristics" (Strawson 39). That is, the particulars that constitute this framework must have the same properties that the framework is to have. As Strawson states earlier, these properties are those which constitute a spatio-temporal framework, i.e. a framework with "one temporal and three spatial dimensions" (38). Thus, the particulars which are to constitute this framework must be three-dimensional and endure through time.[11] And as one might assume, these particulars also have to be observable if they are to constitute our framework. Strawson concludes that "of the categories of objects which we recognize, only those satisfy these requirements which are, or possess, material bodies-in a broad sense of the expression. Material bodies constitute the framework" (39).

After establishing that material bodies constitute this framework and are therefore the basic particulars, Strawson addresses the issue that in order for the framework to be continuously usable, we must be able to *reidentify* the basic particulars that constitute the framework.[12] Strawson argues that material objects are the only type of particulars that we are able to reidentify without reference to other particulars. In order for us to reidentify particulars, they must exist through time, and this requires that they exist through space. Thus, the same criteria that material objects fulfilled in establishing themselves as constituents of the framework and, hence, basic particulars has allowed them the reidentifiability necessary to uphold the framework.

To ground this argument, for the sake of concreteness and clarification, Strawson creates a series of specific arguments, two of which I will examine. First, I will consider one of Strawson's more controversial examples concerning identifiability-dependence. Strawson provides us with the examples of a strike or a lock-out. Strawson explicates, "The possession of the concepts under which such particulars fall all too evidently presupposes the possession of other concepts under which fall particulars of wholly different and far less sophisticated types" (44). Thus, our concept of a strike relies on the concepts of tools, men and women, and perhaps a factory. Strawson believes that the general identifiability-dependence of more sophisticated particulars relies upon the identifiability of more specific particulars "of *wholly different* and far less sophisticated types" (44).[13] These sophisticated particulars, e.g. an event, rely upon *basic* particulars. This, of course, is not to say that in every occasion of discussing more sophisticated particulars, e.g. a football game, we must refer to the less sophisticated *basic* particulars. We may talk of a football game without ever mentioning the football.

The second argument Strawson puts forth, which will attempt to answer his original question concerning asymmetry, is of a more theoretical nature. Many believe that the majority, if not all, events, states, and processes have to be events, states, and process *of* something or somethings. Furthermore, this thing or these things must not be events, states, or processes, but basic particulars. Strawson elaborates:

> It might be thought that from this fact alone it could be argued directly that the identification of most events, states or processes must proceed *via* the identification of those particulars of other types to the history of which they belonged; that e.g. where a particular event was of a kind such that all events of this kind necessarily happen to things of another type, then the identification of the particular

> event necessarily involved the identification of the particular thing to which it happened. (50)

So if this type of argument works, it is impossible to make reference to an event without at least implicitly making reference to the object(s) of the event. For instance, if I am to talk of a birth, under this position, then I must be talking about the birth of something, the birth of *this*. Talking of a birth would entail talking about the birth of this creature. Strawson feels this position is unacceptable and necessarily flawed: "The original argument errs in trying to infer from a conceptual dependence too direct a kind of identifiability-dependence of particulars" (Strawson 51). Strawson provides us with the example of a scream and a screamer. It is quite possible to make reference to a scream without mentioning the screamer. This is not to say, however, that the scream isn't dependent on the screamer, just that it can be identified independently of it. A weaker proposal is necessary. Strawson suggests:

> Suppose that βs are necessarily βs of αs (e.g. that births are necessarily births of animals). Then, though on a particular occasion I may identify a particular β without identifying the α it is of, yet it would not in general be possible to identify βs unless it were in general possible to identify αs. For we could not speak of βs as we do speak of them, or have the concept we do have of βs, unless we spoke of αs; and we could not speak of αs unless it were in principle possible to identify an α. So, in a general sense, βs show identifiability-dependence on αs. (51)

Strawson is worried, and rightfully so, that at first glance his weakened form of the theoretical argument may be taken to show a symmetrical relation between objects and events. For instance, to use Strawson's example, if we hold that the concept we have of a birth entails the concept we have of an animal, then the concept we have of an animal must entail the concept we have of a birth. Consider the following example:

(1) *This is a birth.*
entails
(2) *There is some animal of which this is the birth.*

and

(3) *This is an animal.*
entails
(4) *There is some birth which is the birth of this animal.*

While this relationship seems to be symmetrical, Strawson asks us to press on and find suitable paraphrases of the two entailments. While (3) and (4) can be paraphrased as follows:

(3') *This is an animal.*
entails
(4') *This was born.*

there is no suitable paraphrase for (1)'s entailment of (2). Why is this? Strawson holds that while in our discourse our conception of an animal requires that it be *born*, it does not necessitate that "we must *also* find a place in our discourse for the idea of a certain range of particulars, viz. births" (52). Since I have lost faith in my ability to properly explain this argument, I will quote Strawson's defense of it:

> . . . the admission into our discourse of the range of particulars, *births*, conceived of as we conceive of them, does require the admission into our discourse of the range of particulars, *animals*; but the admission into our discourse of the range of particulars, *animals*, conceived of as we conceive of them, does not require the admission into our discourse of the range of particulars, *births*. (52)

Moravcsik's Critique: Asymmetry Lost?

As Moravcsik allows in Part Three of his essay, "Strawson and Ontological Priority", "Let us assume that the notion of particular-identification is at least intuitively clear ... Can we accept Strawson's claim that among these types [particulars], with respect to the relation specified, material bodies are prior to all other types?" (114). As we shall see, Moravcsik's criticism of Strawson will have two purposes: first, to challenge the claim that material objects are basic particulars, and second, to verify that no other particulars enjoy an equal or a more basic status. Moravcsik elaborates:

> In other words, Strawson has to show not only that there is no asymmetrical dependency which shows material bodies to be posterior, but also that there is no other type which has a mutual, symmetrical dependency relation with material bodies. ... I shall argue that such a symmetrical relationship does hold between material bodies and types of event, actions, and process.[14] (114)

I will first give an exposition of Moravcsik's critique of two of Strawson's general arguments followed by his critique of two of Strawson's specific arguments.

Moravcsik first attacks the criterion Strawson holds as necessary for particulars to possess in order to constitute his framework and thus be considered basic. As we can recall, Strawson believes that basic particulars must be located in space and time and must endure through time. Furthermore, Strawson says that these particulars must be locatable in our four-dimensional framework, consisting of three spatial dimensions and one temporal dimension. Moravcsik protests the need to have three dimensions as part of the criterion for identifiability: "Once ... the condition of three-dimensionality is dropped, events, actions and processes become as good candidates for basicness as are material bodies" (115). Moravcsik proceeds by asserting that "some events, actions and processes have as much stability in space and time as any material body has, even though the question of dimensionality does not arise in connection with them" (115). Moravcsik provides no support for this position nor does he suggest how many dimensions he thinks are necessary as a criterion of identifying events or objects. However, Moravcsik admits that this is a negative argument and by itself will not persuade us to consider events as basic particulars.

Strawson's other criterion for basic particulars, viz. endurance through time, is the subject of Moravcsik's second attack. Strawson states:

> ... a condition, in turn, of the possession of a single, continuously usable framework of this kind, was the ability to *re*identify at least some elements of the framework in spite of discontinuities of observation: that is to say, one must be able to identify some particular things as *the same again* as those encountered on a previous occasion. (55)

This is to say that we must be able to identify an entity E at time t and at a later time t'. Strawson goes on to say that as far as particulars are concerned, material objects are the only type of particular which we can identify in this fashion without reference to other types of particulars. Moravcsik attempts to provide that the re-identification of material objects requires reference to events, and granting that the opposite is true, that their identification dependency, and hence ontological priority, is symmetrical.[15] Moravcsik first argues that if we need to re-identify material objects, we will have to locate two different times that the body inhabits; and reference to times involves a reference to events.[16] This argument is elaborated by identifying these events as observations. In order to re-identify, we would need to observe something twice. For example, I might say "This lamp looks like the one I saw yesterday." Such a statement would suggest that I performed an observation of the lamp yesterday, i.e. an event, and performed a second observation of the lamp right now. Moravcsik concludes:

> Thus the re-identification of material bodies depends on reference to events, and even though the identification of these may depend in some ways on the identification of material bodies, this latter dependency makes the relation simply a symmetrical one, rather than something asymmetrical. (116)

Moravcsik finds the same fundamental flaw in Strawson's arguments dealing with specific types. We can take the example used earlier in which Strawson holds that 'sophisticated' particulars like strikes or lock-outs require the existence of smaller, basic particulars, i.e. material objects. Strawson asserts that it's hard to imagine a strike without imagining workers, tools, and a factory. Moravcsik replies to this assertion that it can be said that we couldn't have our workers, tools, and a factory without the concepts of production and manufacturing. Someone may counter this by saying, "Yes, but those particulars of production and manufacturing aren't necessary for us to identify the tools and factory, whereas if we didn't have the basic particulars of the tools, factory, and workers, we couldn't identify the strike at all." Moravcsik would counter this counter-attack by referring us back to his previous argument that links identifying with observing, producing a symmetrical ontological relationship.

Moravcsik's final criticism of Strawson concerns his entailment argument concerning births and animals. I believe Moravcsik rightfully points out that "Strawson's ... argument involving specific types seems to rest on drawing illegitimate conclusions from what are contingent features of the English language" (117). If we were to assume that Strawson's argument worked according to his defense of it, then only material objects would hold an ontological priority over events and asymmetry would be upheld. Moravcsik offers an analogous argument to point out the absurdity of Strawson's argument:

(5) *This is an occasion of eating.*
entails
(6) *There is an animal which eats on this occasion.*

and

(7) *This is an animal.*
entails
(8) *There are occasions on which this animal eats.*

Moravcsik says that Strawson would have to hold that we can paraphrase (7)'s entailment of (8) as:

(7') *This is an animal.*
entails
(8') *This animal is an eater.*

without admitting to the existence of an occasion of eating. Moravcsik concludes, "Frankly, I can make no sense out of the concept of an eater which does not involve occasions of eating, and thus I fail to see how the alleged asymmetry would hold" (118). Moravcsik's example reveals the fact that it is merely a feature of the English language that allows Strawson to complete his example concerning 'a birth' and 'an animal being born'. While I agree with Moravcsik that this was a bad example, I agree only with the fact that it is a bad example. Most of Strawson's argument can be salvaged after a necessary distinction is made.

A Distinction

While I have only alluded to certain distinctions concerning weak dependencies, a line has to be drawn between weak and strong dependencies. All of Moravcsik's objections to Strawson's position on events are solid objections; however, they fail to make mention of a subtle distinction that will have the result of putting most of Moravcsik's objections in the arena of weak dependence. The distinction I will make is between *what is involved in the identification of particulars* and *what is involved in the identification process*. As mentioned earlier, the foundational dependencies I placed under the title of weak dependencies were not of great importance in the relationship between the event and object at hand. In other words, we are interested in the individuation criterion we need to identify events and objects and not the events and objects involved in identifying and individuating these events, i.e. observations and observers. The dependency relations between objects and events we are concerned with are *strong* dependencies. Strong dependency is the dependence that the objects and events *at hand* exert over each other, regardless of historical relations, or our observation of them. Strong dependency can be additionally, and more rigidly, defined as such: an object or event is dependent in a strong sense on an event or object, respectively, when the disappearance of latter would eliminate the former *at some level*. The levels I will be concerned with in my later discussion of Strawson will be ontological and conceptual.

By examining Moravcsik's four arguments in light of this distinction, we may properly categorize his objections into our weak or strong categories of dependence. Moravcsik's first argument is not one to worry about, since he provides no support of its claim that the framework criterion does not need to be three-dimensional. Moravcsik's second argument succumbs to the overlooked distinction. Moravcsik states, "For in order to raise questions about the re-identification of any material body, we have to locate two segments of time which the body allegedly occupied and occupies" (116). While this is true, he has collapsed the distinction concerning the criterion which makes possible both the identification of the objects possible, and *our* identification of them. This is not to deny the importance of our identification process, but it is, nevertheless, accounted for and would not create what we call a strong dependence. What we are concerned with in the re-identification of objects is their properties, i.e. their shape, three dimensionality, etc., that allows them to be re-identified. In short, we are concerned with what is necessary to be *able* to identify and re-identify objects and not the identifying and re-identifying of them itself.

This same critique follows for the first of Moravcsik's two specific arguments against specific types. The history of the objects in the strike and the events involved in manufacturing them is accounted for within the weak dependency category, and is not, as Moravcsik foresees that Strawson might claim, necessary to the identification of sophisticated particulars. Since Moravcsik's defense of this position is the same as the one for his previous argument, supposedly forcing symmetry, we may look to the argument just stated above to answer this.

It is necessary to point out the flaw in Moravcsik's claim that historically-regressive dependency creates a symmetrical dependence with material objects, denying them the status of basic particulars. Historically-regressive dependence has been shown to be a weak dependency because, to put it crudely, the events and objects involved in historically-regressive dependence are not immediately involved in the event. In fact, historically-regressive dependencies are involved in their own events in which it would not be problematic if the object of observation played a small role. This is, nevertheless, irrelevant. Things like a smiler smiling do not rely in any *strong* way on things like me observing the smile or, for the smiler, the smiler's mother and father. What Moravcsik is trying to do is create a *crosscategorical symmetrical dependence* between things that are involved in strong dependency relationships and things that are involved in weak dependency relationships.

The final argument to which Moravcsik replies is a strange one. While I am sympathetic and in agreement with his analysis of Strawson's entailment argument, that, unfortunately for Moravcsik, does not end the issue. I believe Strawson's argument is faulty and even under the assumption that the argument went through, it would do nothing more than prove an asymmetrical dependence between animals and births in the English language. Furthermore, we can see here that Strawson falls into the same trap as Moravcsik by mistakenly trying to maintain and equate a cross-categorical dependency with a strong dependency. Strawson's motivation behind the argument, however, is quite solid and still open for debate.

Asymmetry Regained

Strawson is on the mark in exploring the issue of asymmetry he felt existed between the basic particulars, i.e. material objects, and events. Strawson continues in his critique that the general argument is too strong in creating a symmetrical dependence (50). Recall, "The original argument errs in trying to infer from conceptual dependence too direct a kind of identifiability-dependence of particulars" (51). We may continue from here with an example that leaves out the history of a certain class of material objects, e.g. the births of creatures.[17] Let's imagine an example that doesn't explicitly entertain weak dependencies:

(9) *The smile had a smiler.*
and
(10) *The smiler had a smile.*[18]

To draw out the inherent qualities of these examples, we may restate (9) and (10) in the following fashion:

(9') *The event had an object.*
and
(10') *The object had an event.*

Thus, in (10) and (10') if we were to eliminate the object, in an ontological way, i.e. the object disappears, we would eliminate the event. Therefore, there can't be a smile without a smiler. However, if we look at (9) and (9') and choose to get rid of the event in the same ontological way, i.e. the event disappears, the smiler nevertheless seems to leave an object, let's say Jones, which still exists. When we get rid of the smile, we get rid of the smiler, but not the individual. From this we might say that in a strong sense events are *ontologically* dependent on objects whereas objects are only *conceptually* dependent on events. To explain this further, when we describe objects in terms of an event associated with them, a smile and a smiler or a scream and a screamer, the description of the individual as a smiler or screamer is dependent on the circumstance that the individual performs the event required of his or her description, i.e. smiling or screaming. If the individual does not on occasion perform the event that allows for a particular object description, setting aside gray areas, then that description no longer applies. The description of a smiler or screamer is dependent on the concept, and event, of smiling or screaming. Therefore, the relation between events and objects is asymmetrical: a strong ontological dependence of events on objects, and a strong conceptual dependence of objects on events.

The arguments between Strawson and Moravcsik have allowed us to discover and identify different categories of dependency as well as categorize the role they play in event-object relations. These clarifications have, for the most part, provided support for Strawson's view on asymmetrical dependency between events and objects. While I am not committing myself to Strawson's views concerning objects, the purpose of this discussion was to show that it stands up to Moravcsik's criticism.

NOTES

1. An extended version of this paper appears under the title "Asymmetrical and Symmetrical Dependency: A Particular Problem" in *Aporia*, Volume 6: 1996.

2. I believe P. F. Strawson's *Individuals* really brought the debate concerning the ontological commitments between events and objects into full swing. This will be my earliest reference concerning the issue.

3. While there is much controversy as to what events are, I find the case against the existence of events to be fairly weak. Hacker appropriately responds: "The *esse* of events is to take place, happen or occur, but not to exist. ... At worst the question of whether events exist should be answered in the negative, not because events do not exist (like unicorns), but because it is senseless to say of events either that they exist or that they do not" (479). One could think of asking whether or not objects occur as a similar question. Nevertheless, charity will allow us to construe events as existing for sake of the discussion.

4. The term 'weak' is a bit misleading. I consider these ontological dependencies to be foundational. Nevertheless, I consider these dependencies to be of little philosophical interest, and, therefore, lacking the strength of what I will later call *strong* ontological dependencies.

5. I will take events to be Events with a capital 'E', to include processes and states as well as events. Hacker might disagree with my inclusion of states as Events.

6. When discussing our world, we may allow the fact that we do measure time by change and space by objects. We know this through our observations, but that is not to say that observations, not to confuse with observability, play a role in our discussion at this moment.

7. This tracing of observations to observers, which are people, back to births, and further back to parents is the type of switch-off between objects and events that presents an infinite regress, which isn't very interesting to say the least.

8. These weak dependencies are: 1) spatial and temporal dependencies as described in the concrete world examples, and 2) historically-regressive dependencies. While the first type of dependencies are clearly symmetrical, I have doubts as to whether we can call historically-regressive dependencies fully symmetrical due to the infinite regress.

9. This is an innocent usage of three dimensionality and should not be looked upon as excluding events from the running for basic particulars. Three dimensional space is merely the space part of the spatio-temporal framework Strawson plans to explore.

10. Strawson's framework is not a conceptual structure containing different particulars, but a framework composed *of* basic particulars.

11. I think Strawson may be sympathetic with the idea that basic particulars merely have to exist at some time and not necessarily endure *through* it.

12. Strawson makes many arguments defending his view that material bodies are basic particulars (39-54) which are too numerous to mention here. I will, nevertheless, invoke some of them later in light of Moravcsik's criticisms.

13. Italics added.

14. Two clarifications must be added. First, Moravcsik will be continuing the theme I have been using by talking about events with a capital 'E' as including states and processes as well. Second, I will present Moravcsik's criticisms of Strawson in the same order that Strawson's arguments were presented.

15. Moravcsik holds earlier in this article that "[Strawson's] formula ties ontological priority to dependence with respect to identifiability" (108).

16. We can recall and rework Hacker's arguments to show this. A reference to time is possible because there is a change, for that is how we know time progresses. Such a change would be an event.

17. I am not altogether sure that Strawson was overtly aware of the distinction I drew above. Nevertheless, the birth and animal argument is the only place he seems to skew this issue.

18. Thanks to Achille Varzi for the example.

References

Hacker, P. M. S. "Events, Ontology and Grammar." *Philosophy* 57 (1982): 477-86.

Moravcsik, J. M. E. "Strawson and Ontological Priority." *Analytical Philosophy*. R. J. Butler (editor). 2nd ser. New York: Barnes and Noble, 1968: 106-119.

Strawson, P. F. *Individuals: An Essay in Descriptive Metaphysics*. London: Menthuen/Routledge, 1959.

Philosophical Journeys of Self and Spirit

FOLLOW YOUR BLISS: THE PHILOSOPHY OF JOSEPH CAMPBELL

Angela Case
Le Moyne College

In 1988, the year after his death, Joseph Campbell entranced thousands of Americans who tuned in to PBS to watch *The Hero's Journey: The World of Joseph Campbell* as well as the six hour interview series, *The Power of Myth*, conducted by journalist Bill Moyers. Throughout the course of these conversations the Professor of Mythology shared his insight on topics spanning from initiation rituals of the aborigines in Australia to the movie *Star Wars*. But the idea Campbell returns to over and over again is the mystery that pervades human life, reminding audiences that "Life is not a problem to be solved but a mystery to be lived."[1] Campbell explains this mystery as the ultimate impersonal energy source which brings life into being and stores within all creation the potential for making life meaningful. Thus throughout his work, Campbell contends, the journey of human life is the quest to establish connection with the life source energy found within all beings, followed by the struggle to live life in accordance with our own unique potentialities.

The philosophy Campbell proposes to assure we experience the "fulfillment of our own potentialities"[2] is "follow your bliss". This loaded phrase suggests that by living the life destined to be our own, we will know the greatest amount of happiness and inner peace possible. Campbell explains, "if you do follow your bliss you put yourself on a kind of track that has been there all the while, waiting for you, and the life that you ought to be living is the one you are living."[3] Throughout our lifetime, Campbell argues, our experiences and our relationships with others provide glimpses of our bliss. Grabbing onto these "pangs of the heart", Campbell asserts, is the first step on the human journey that ensures our actions in "the purely physical plane will have resonances within our innermost being."[4]

Campbell developed his philosophy for living through his study of mythology. As a young boy, a trip to Buffalo Bill's Wild West Show at Madison Square Garden followed by a visit to the Museum of Natural History sparked Campbell's interest in Native Americans and mythology. His fascination pushed him to read all he could about American Indians and through his studies Campbell discovered comparisons between the native myths and legends and the stories of his own Roman Catholic religion. This initial interest in comparative mythology eventually led Campbell to abandon work on his Ph.D. and dedicate his life to exploring the origins of myths, explaining how myths speak to us and demonstrating the impact they have on our lives. Through his work Campbell discovered that the key to "following your bliss" was actually living a "mythologically grounded life."[5]

In *The Hero's Journey*, Campbell says "My definition of myth now is: a metaphor transparent to transcendence," explaining that "mythology opens the world so that it becomes transparent to something that is beyond speech, beyond word, in short, to that what we call transcendence."[6] The "something" Campbell refers to is the mysterious life source energy which gives rise to human existence, yet exists in a realm beyond the scope of human comprehension. Through his definition Campbell asserts that, although myths struggle to uncover the mystery of the transcendent in their attempts to answer fundamental questions about the origins of the world and explain the meaning of life and death, ultimately these stories reveal no answers exist. Campbell refers to this as the first of the four functions of mythology, the mystical function, which is responsible for "opening the heart and mind, pointing out that the ultimate mystery that we all try to solve lies beyond the range of human thought or naming."[7] Campbell also suggests the second function of mythology, the cosmological dimension, supports the notion of mythology's struggle to deal with the sublime in its efforts to explain the unexplainable forces that shape the universe. Therefore, Campbell argues, myths do not reveal ultimate truths: instead they embody the Sanskrit idea that "He who thinks he knows, doesn't know. He who knows he doesn't know, knows."[8]

The origins of myths rest in the desire of the human mind to explain "the deepest hopes, desires, and fears, potentialities and conflicts of human will."[9] Combining studies of biology and psychoanalysis Campbell proposes that myths arise from the human imagination's attempts to explain the three primal biological urges shared by all human beings — life eating life, the desire to reproduce, and the desire for possession. Although these energies are what Campbell refers to as "the essence of life itself" he warns that when unchecked these forces "become terrific, horrifying, and destructive."[10] Therefore, myths attempt to explain why human beings share these bestial impulses. Campbell infuses psychoanalysis into his explanation of the origins of myths, referring to Carl Jung's notion of the "collective unconscious" which suggests that, as human beings, "the energies that inform the body are energies that inform our dreams."[11] The repetition of mythic images used to explain biological urges across cultural boundaries demonstrate the commonality of human existence.

Campbell cites the universal nature of myths as the true power of mythology. The fact that myths reveal that human biology is everywhere the same, as well as demonstrating that the mystery of what it means to be human is a struggle all humans share, illustrates the interconnectedness of all humanity. In one instance Campbell demonstrates the similarities that exist among various mythologies by reading stories of creation from the book of *Genesis*, the *Upanishads*, and legends from Native American Indian mythology side by side and illustrating how each tells the same story.[12] While emphasizing the common aspects of mythology, Campbell does not deny the local or tribal quality of all myths. Campbell defines the third or sociological function of mythology as the use of myths by a society to "support and validate a certain social order" and thus "myths vary enormously from place to place."[13] Campbell also suggests that because myths arise from the human imagination which depends upon the immediate physical world for sources of comparison, myths differ. Yet, he contends, when looking at the similarities of the over-arching themes in mythology, the universal quality surely outweighs the presence of these differences.

The power of this universality of myths lies in the fact that it puts us in touch with others struggling to unravel the mystery and thus provides us with a sense of hope. As individuals embarking on the journey of human life to seek and to know bliss, myths furnish models of others who have taken the journey and grant the comfort of knowing we are not alone. The fourth function of mythology, the pedagogical or teaching function, enforces this power of myth by suggesting myths teach what it means to be human and become examples necessary to learn "how to live a human life"[14] reflective of that humanity. Thus, Campbell believes myths encourage us to take the first step on the path of following bliss.

Campbell's study of mythology focused most intently on the adventures of heroes and the vision quest, for he found these stories to be perfect models of the human journey of "following your bliss". In his first book, *The Hero With a Thousand Faces*, Campbell suggests that all hero myths follow the same basic pattern: separation — initiation — return, that he names the monomyth. The journey begins when the "hero ventures forth from the world of common day into a world of supernatural wonder."[15] The hero's "crossing of the threshold" or movement from the known world into depths unexplored is analogous to forging out on the human adventure. Although Campbell is clear that this movement onto the path of bliss can occur at any time in life, rites of passage associated with adolescence suggest that the journey most frequently begins during this time of newfound independence. The transition from childhood dependence to adult responsibilities requires we make many decisions that will impact the rest of our lives. Campbell suggests that by turning inward and listening to the heart when making these life choices, one sets out into the unknown to discover the true life waiting to be our own independent of the influence of others.

Another model Campbell discovered which effectively symbolizes the human journey to seek and then to follow bliss is the psychological transformations that occur during the practice of yoga. In *The Inner Reaches of Outer Space*, Campbell explains the movement through physical chakras as a metaphor for transformations along the journey to higher planes of consciousness. The first step of the yogic practice is the movement beyond the first three chakras, located in the pelvic region, because of their association with the animalistic rather than human, and movement into chakra 4, the region of the heart. The awakening that occurs is, according to Campbell, "the beginning of humanity". At this moment we abandon bestial urges and enter into the unknown region of the heart, which is ruled by feelings of love and compassion. Therefore, living a life in accordance with chakra 4 we begin exploring those feelings which make us human and by following them we seek the bliss that the heart points us towards.

Campbell does not deny the difficulties associated with taking the first step and beginning the adventure. To leave the protective walls of home and enter into the region of the unknown is a frightening proposition. Campbell suggests that as hero myths demonstrate, some willingly take up the challenge, and some "walled in boredom, hard work or 'culture'"[16] refuse to take the journey altogether. Still others, Campbell illustrates, do not intend to begin the adventure; but the arrival of a "herald figure" lures them onto the path.[17] Campbell argues the "herald figure" symbolizes those experiences and people we meet that begin to expose the potentialities we possess and encourage us to set out on the adventure.

Embarking on the journey is only to overcome the first obstacle. Challenges to living an authentic human life continue to present themselves all along the path. Just as the hero must slay dragons and monsters and resist temptation along the way, so too must individuals on the journey be wary of the "human fantasies"[18] which try to hold the spirit back. Campbell associates these "human fantasies" with the three primal biological urges, most especially the desire for possession. This attaches value to power, wealth, and fame and leads us astray from following the callings of the heart, preventing us from ever realizing our bliss. The yogic model illustrates the difficulty suggesting it may take months or years of practice before an individual can successfully move beyond the first three chakras and come to know the energies of the heart.

Campbell associates the "crossing of the threshold" in his own life with the crisis of faith that occurred when his study of Biology collided with the teachings of the Roman Catholic tradition in which he was raised. Campbell compared his own experience to that of Stephen Dedalus, the hero in James Joyce's novel, *A Portrait of the Artist as a Young Man*. The novel traces Stephen's attempt to free himself from the confining nets of family, nation, and religion in order to find the independent voice of the artist. Relating Stephen's journey to his own life, Campbell explains,

> ... his problem was my problem, exactly. And the problem is when you're deeply built into a system of the church and you're losing your faith it's no fun ... there's absolutely no relationship between biological evolution of the human species, the animal and the plant world and what you get in the Book of Genesis.[19]

Campbell's struggle to explain these discrepancies between the spiritual and the scientific worlds marked the start of his own journey. Thus, when Campbell describes his philosophy, he speaks from personal experience, understanding the frustrations that can occur while in the midst of the adventure.

In spite of the frustrations and difficulties the hero faces along the way, Campbell repeatedly reminds us that the hero does not undertake the journey alone. Figures such as the Spider Woman in American Indian mythology, the old crone that frequently appears in fairy tales, as well as angels or fairies present in other myths represent the powers available to help the hero overcome obstacles. In terms of the human adventure, Campbell suggests, these guiding forces symbolize those that have taken the journey before us and represent the "protective power [that] is always and ever present within the sanctuary of the heart and even immanent within or just behind the unfamiliar features of the world. One only has to know and trust and the ageless guardians will appear."[20] The symbolic value of these supernatural aids embody the entire notion of the power of myth which connects the individual to the universal. They demonstrate the fact that the journey is a human journey and provide the hope needed to advance on the path of discovery.

Along with the encouragement provided by the knowledge that others have taken the journey prior to ourselves, Campbell maintains that hope is also furnished by the fact that we do not enter the sphere of the unknown without a purpose; we are seeking the key to the mystery in an attempt to answer the question, "Who am I?". Campbell reminds us that myths tell us no answers exist; the energy that gives us life transcends knowing or understanding. Various myths choose to give names to that transcendent quality: God, Buddha, Allah, Presence, the Divine, and so on, but ultimately all refer to the same thing: the mysterious life source which pervades all beings and thus connects all creation. Therefore, the goal of the journey, the thing we are seeking, is not an explanation of the mystery, but an understanding that the ultimate truth is a mystery. Experiencing the mystery is the experience of bliss, or what Campbell refers to as the moment of the "Aha!".

In mythic terms Campbell suggests the "ultimate boon" of the hero's adventure is often a reunion with the hero's lost Father, the source of life. On a figurative level the Father becomes the transcendent life source energy all seek when embarking on the human journey. Campbell calls the moment of connection "at-one-ment" suggesting that "the son who has really grown to know the father ... the world is no longer a vale of tears but a bliss-yielding, perpetual manifestation of the Presence."[21] The hero experiences enlightenment realizing the existence of the life source within and knowing bliss.

In the practice of yoga connection with the mysterious occurs during the movement to chakra 7 located at the crown of the head. Here the individual experiences "a rapture beyond any god known as a name or form"[22] and in this moment of transcendence one realizes that the sublime energies exist not only within the Self but also throughout the whole of creation. In Buddhist tradition, Campbell points out, the belief that "All things are Buddha things!" summarizes this awareness of the interconnectedness of all beings and celebrates the sacred nature of all creation.

The heart of Campbell's philosophy of living an authentic human life occurs in the next phase of the adventure. After having experienced a moment of bliss and knowing the ultimate connection that exists between all creation, Campbell suggests the next step is the transformation of the journey from one of seeking to one of following bliss where it leads. Knowing bliss for Campbell is not the end but rather the beginning of a new and more exciting portion of the journey.

Campbell's discussion of the second half of the journey remains ambiguous because no one explanation suffices. A key aspect of "following your bliss" is that "your" bliss is distinct from all others. "What is unknown is the fulfillment of your own unique life, the likes of which have never existed on earth. And you are the only one who can do it," Campbell explains, "people can give you clues how to fall down and how to stand up: but when to fall and when you are standing, this only you can know."[23] The paths of bliss, therefore, are as numerous as the individuals embarking on the journey.

Campbell remains clear about two aspects of the second portion of the journey. First he insists that the journey must continue and, more importantly, that the remainder of the adventure must entail living a life of compassion which acknowledges the interconnectedness of humanity experienced during the first half of the adventure. Campbell argues that, because we live in the physical realm of being, suffering exists and is inescapable. "Life is pain," he writes, "but compassion is what gives it the possibility of continuing."[24] Campbell literally translates compassion to mean "suffering with."[25] He contends that the interdependence we experience throughout the journey awakens the heart to shared human suffering and teaches service to others as the means of survival. Thus Campbell asserts, "the ultimate aim of the quest must be neither release nor ecstacy for oneself, but the wisdom and power to serve others."[26]

In the hero's adventure, the second half of the journey begins when the hero returns to the society from which he or she originally departed. Campbell writes, "the norm of the monomyth, requires that the hero shall now begin the labor of bringing the ruins of wisdom, the Golden Fleece, or his sleeping princess back into the kingdom of humanity, where the boon may redound to the renewing of the community, the nation, the planet, or the ten thousand worlds."[27] Thus, whether the hero willingly rejoins the community, or the society who is "jealous of those who remain away from it"[28] forces the hero to return, he or she must re-enter the realm of the social world to share the knowledge gained with the community.

Attempting to share with others the wisdom acquired throughout the adventure is "the hero's ultimate difficult task. How to render back into the light-world the speech defying pronouncements of the dark?"[29] Often, Campbell points out, the hero appears giant among others because the knowledge gained along the way raises the hero to a level of consciousness far beyond those who have not yet embarked on the adventure.[30] Yet, Campbell maintains if the hero is to be a final success, he or she must accept the role of the "teaching savior" and share the mystery with others.

The yogic model suggests that after having experienced enlightenment at chakra 7, individuals return to chakra 4 and live life in accordance with the human cares and concerns of the heart. Spiritual Wanderers of Eastern traditions choose to live life in accordance with chakra 7 and abandon society altogether to live in a realm of bliss for the remainder of their lifetime. Campbell rejects this life choice of world renunciation because of his belief that those who have begun the journey should return to society and share the wisdom they have gained. He argues that by returning to chakra 4, the realm of the awakened heart, compassion replaces "bestial self-interest"[31] and sharing knowledge of the adventure with others becomes a primary concern.

His own path of bliss led Campbell to the secluded area of Woodstock, NY where he dedicated five years of his life to reading. Campbell admitted to spending nine to twelve hours a day exploring the mystery he found in the works of Carl Jung, Thomas Mann, James Joyce and countless others. Understanding the mystery found within these pages was not the end but the start of his own journey. Following the model he discovered, Campbell abandoned the isolation of his Woodstock home and rejoined the ranks of society to share the wealth of knowledge he had accumulated with others. Thus, he began his thirty-eight year teaching career at Sarah Lawrence College and the publication of twenty books. By accepting the role of the "teaching savior" Campbell's own life became the embodiment of the hero's journey that he spent the majority of his time studying.

Campbell argues that those who refuse the call to embark on the journey live in what T. S. Elliot referred to as "The Waste Land" and doom themselves to a death-in-life type of existence.[32] Chained to primal urges, these individuals allow convention, individualism and material concerns to replace the calls of the heart. They ignore their own potentialities and instead conform to the demands of others. Recounting a conversation overheard in a restaurant one evening, Campbell tells of a man admitting to his family in despair that he had never done a thing he wanted to his entire life. Campbell suggests that the man condemned himself to the prison of the "waste land" because he never embarked on the journey of following bliss which Campbell maintains is necessary in order to live a life of true happiness and fulfillment.[33]

Campbell contends that life in the "waste land" is a more frightening proposition then actual physical death. For, he argues, the "peak experience" of bliss, the moment when we establish connection with "the energy of the universe of which all things are manifestations,"[34] occurs during the journey of human life and not, as some religious traditions claim, after we have died. Therefore, Campbell asserts, "the adventure is its own reward,"[35] suggesting that if we do not embark on the journey of following our bliss we will never know the "rapture of being alive"[36] and our life in this world passes without purpose or meaning.

NOTES

1. *The Hero's Journey*, p. xiv.
2. *The Power of Myth*, p. 151.
3. *Ibid.*, p. 120.
4. *Ibid.*, p. 5.
5. *An Open Life*, p. 24.
6. *The Hero's Journey*, p. 40.
7. *Ibid.*, p. 162.
8. *The Power of Myth*, p. 55.
9. *The Inner Reaches of Outer Space*, p. 55.
10. *Ibid.*, p. 13.
11. *The Hero's Journey*, p. 45.
12. *The Power of Myth*, pp. 24-54.
13. *Ibid.*, p. 31.
14. *Ibid.*
15. *The Hero With a Thousand Faces*, p. 30.
16. *Ibid.*, p. 59.
17. *Ibid.*, p. 51.
18. *Ibid.*, p. 11.
19. *The Hero's Journey*, p. 28.
20. *The Hero With a Thousand Faces*, pp. 71-72.
21. *Ibid.*, p. 148.

22. *The Inner Reaches of Outer Space*, p. 65.

23. *An Open Life*, p. 76.

24. *The Power of Myth*, p. 160.

25. *Ibid.*

26. *Ibid.*, p. xv.

27. *The Hero With a Thousand Faces*, p. 193.

28. *Ibid.*, p. 207.

29. *Ibid.*, p. 218.

30. *The Hero's Journey*, p. 196.

31. *The Power of Myth*, p. 160.

32. *Ibid.*, p. 131.

33. *Ibid.*, p. 118.

34. *Ibid.*, p. 230.

35. *Ibid.*, p. 158.

36. *Ibid.*, p. 5.

References

Joseph Campbell. *The Hero's Journey: The World of Joseph Campbell*. Phil Cousineau (editor). San Francisco: Harper and Row, 1990.

Joseph Campbell. *The Hero With a Thousand Faces*. New York: Bollingen Foundation, 1949.

Joseph Campbell. *The Inner Reaches of Outer Space: Metaphor as Myth and as Religion*. New York: Harper and Row, 1986.

Joseph Campbell and Bill Moyers. *The Power of Myth*. Betty Sue Flowers (editor). New York: Doubleday, 1988.

Joseph Campbell and Michael Toms. *An Open Life: Joseph Campbell in Conversation with Michael Toms*. John M. Maher and Dennie Briggs (editors). New York: Larsen Publications, 1988.

Concepts of Self: East and West

Gabrielle Levin
SUNY - Oneonta

The Self. How can we begin to define it? How pretentious of us to think that we have found the answer. The concept of self is both complex and abstract. The study of the self, as one might imagine, can become very controversial and argumentative.

Cross-culturally, the concept of self can come to mean very different things and, as we shall see, the roles of the members of the same culture will vary due to differences such as gender or status in the hierarchy. Is the self an innate quality that waits to be discovered? Or is the self solely a matter of cultural influence? The focus of this paper is to investigate the relationships between different Eastern philosophies. When investigating the relationships, two subsidiary questions will arise: (i) "What, if anything, is there for us as Westerners to learn from other concepts of self?" and (ii) "What, if anything, can we teach them?"

Let us try a literal understanding of the self. We begin with the dictionary. We find soon enough that the dictionary will offer us little if any help. The self is defined as "1-The identity, character, etc. of any person or thing, 2-one's own person distinct from others."[1] I am afraid that without some prior concept as to what the self might already be, this definition would do little or nothing to explain the term. The self is being described in terms that pertain to the very preliminary understanding of the self! If we do know something about the self already, then this definition becomes even more of a disappointment. I regret to report that we are "beyond the comforts of the dictionary."[2] To truly understand what the idea of the self entails, it is necessary to take a "more metaphorical rather than ... literal standard."[3]

In order to compare and contrast the different Eastern philosophies, it is helpful to first take a brief look at how these different cultures are related historically. We will also explore how these philosophies have been used, and in some cases even abused, to suit the political needs of a government in power.

* * *

Buddhism originated in India. Socially, India has always had a very rigid caste system. Who you were born to be was who you were for the rest of your life. In this sense, a part of the self is inherited. If you were born poor, chances were you remained poor. If you were fortunate enough to be born powerful and wealthy, well then you must have done something very deserving in your former life.

When the British invaded India, the caste system at first seemed contrary to the British ideal. However, it was a very useful method to the British for controlling purposes. Without the caste system, there would be chaos. The caste system provided order, expectations, and social role in one neat package. So, much to the convenience of the British, the Imperial rule created a more rigid caste system.

From India, Buddhism was transmitted to China where it was filtered through Confucianism and Taoism. As we see later, the concept of self gets in the way. From China, the influence reaches Japan, and we can see its traces in Shinto and Zen. With Zen we again see the negation or extinguishing of the self.

Perhaps the idea of the self in Buddhism can best be described as a 'no-self'. It is considered a mistake to bind yourself with the limitations of the idea of a self. Any differences in self that we might perceive are merely illusory. That is, we perceive the boundaries of our body, but what we need to understand is that this is only a temporal condition. The body is not the essence of the self.

The goal of Buddhism is to let go of the self. Empty the self and you shall become free of all attachment. This is the path to Nirvana or enlightenment. Literally, the term *Nirvana* is often translated as *extinction*. Buddhism teaches that the key to losing yourself is through compassion for others. According to Buddhism. we do not conceptualize pain properly. What we see as independent is actually interdependent. What we must understand is that there is an 'underlying life-force' if you will, that unites all living creatures, and makes us all equal.

Reincarnation is also a key concept in Buddhism. Reincarnation is not a transmigration of the soul, but rather a transference of energy. Consider the metaphor of one candle being used to light another. The process is not the same, but it is parallel. That is to say, my life force may once have been that of Aristotle's, but that is not to say that I am the soul of Aristotle.

As mentioned earlier, India had (and still has today) a very rigid caste system. One would not expect any movement to another level in the system within one's lifetime. Instead, one would accept one's position in society without question. However, it is expected that one will be rewarded for one's virtues in the next life, through reincarnation. If I were born into extreme poverty, it is likely that I would assume that this was the only position I was worthy of, due to my actions in my previous life. However, if I am virtuous in this life, even if I die poor, I will be rewarded for my goodness in the next life. This cycle will repeat itself until I have finally reached nirvana. Buddhism rejects the notion of a persistent self that transmigrates, but accepts the transmigration process and 'karma'. Karma and the caste system go hand in hand.

Karma is an interesting idea that is complicated to explain. Briefly, it is a relationship between cause and effect. Karma is a cosmic principle of linkage over time. Karma helps to explain why things happen the way they do. It helps to explain why we were born who we are. The life we have is a function of the lives we have had. Nothing, according to karma, happens accidentally. If we attempt a western understanding of karma, a theorist such as Sigmund Freud might have said that karma is operating at a subconscious level. To bring karma to a level of consciousness, we use what is the western notion of meditation. The goal of meditation is to see yourself within a larger framework. It is both calming and reassuring to see one's individual self as a larger self. When we meditate, it is as if we experience ourselves in the third person.

The notion that "knowledge of the self gives you the knowledge of everything"[4] is taught in the Upanishads. There is a pragmatic paradox here. In order for something to work, one must believe that it must work. This is true not only for ideas like voodoo, but karma as well.

There needs to be an understanding that losing the self does not mean losing individuality. It means losing the 'false' sense of self. A "false sense of the self is the foci for negative emotion and the liberation from this deception is the path toward the generation of the positive emotions".[5]

Similarities have often been noted between Buddhism and David Hume's notion of the self. On Hume's account, the "self is a fiction, so passions are also fictions ... we are deluded when pride and humility emerge within us".[6] In Buddhism, however, humility is something to be sought and valued. Buddhism teaches that "humility is based on self-confidence, not feelings of inadequacy."[7]

As mentioned earlier, the caste system helped the British to maintain control of India. It has been argued that before the British invasion, the caste system in India was not so rigid and that, in fact, the strict adherence to the system of hierarchy was manifested as a result of the imperial rule. Originally, the caste system was an orderly function that the people of India had accepted. For the British, there was opportunity. The caste system ensured that there would be no autonomy or individuality among the people of India. The caste system rewards behaviors like compliance and punishes autonomy. Clearly, the system was misused by the imperial rule.

* * *

Like Buddhism, Confucianism appeals to people in power. Confucianism basically follows the thought that people need culture and structure because they are not innately good. As we will see later, this differs greatly from Taoism. Confucius, or Kung Fu-Tzu (*tzu* meaning father, teacher, or master) lived in the city. He felt that the self is in the community, and that to have a great person, we need a great community, or environment.

In Confucianism, the body is very important. There is much emphasis on the "ritualization of the body ... (The) body provides the context and the resources for ultimate self-transformation."[8] Confucianism holds that the physical development of the body is the "locus of self-transformation."[9] This leads to the conclusion that personality is achieved rather than given. Confucianism also places high value on feeling empathy for others. To mature "is to accept that to open one's self up is the ceaseless process of human flourishing."[10]

Before the development of Confucianism, China was ruled by many different battling warlords. There was not a single currency. There were also many different languages in China. The notion of one united country at this time was simply fictitious. It is no secret that the causes of war are often greed, a desire for power, and a lack of one unifying power.

Today China is a notoriously collective society. The self is seen as functioning much like a cog in a wheel. The self becomes a mere part of a whole. Even at the early stage of preschool this expectation becomes well learned. Due to over-population, China has adopted a single-child policy. This policy makes it very attractive for couples to only have one child for the greater good of the society. The spoiling of a child would inevitably destroy the values of selflessness and collectivism. Although it has been argued that the one child policy could result in the spoiling of the children, no discernible difference has been found in the rearing of a child in a single child household versus the rearing of a child in a multiple child household.

Even in preschool, children learn "to sacrifice the smaller self to accomplish greater self."[11] Keeping in step with Communism, the teachers are carefully monitored in what they can or cannot teach to the class. The teachers became a useful means through which the ideas of Confucianism and Communism could be instilled at this early age of development. In fact, in China the teacher is often thought to be more influential to the children than their own mother! There is even such a thing as a boarding preschool. "The promotion of selflessness and collectivism lies at the core of the Chinese preschool's mission."[12] Obedience is highly valued and it is important for this notion of collectivism to work.

Whereas Confucius held that the self is in the community, Lao-tzu found the self to be beyond or below the community. Unlike Confucius, Lao-tzu lived in the mountains. He believed that to create an excellent society, we needed to create excellent people. Lao-tzu believed people to be innately good. He believed that governing a country should be much like cooking a small fish: it is best not to overdo it! (This is the concept of *wu-wei*: no action.)

Lao-tzu spoke of a force common to all living and inanimate objects, often called the *Tao*. There are three faces of the Tao. Each one is abstract when considered from the eyes of the western philosopher. With words alone it is difficult to grasp the complete understanding of what is meant by each of these notions. The first face of Tao is the "Tao which cannot be named." This is the unmanifest Tao which is most pure or pristine. It is so pure that it is actually 'nameless'.

The second face of Tao is the 'Manifest Tao'. This is the Tao as it becomes physical (physical space, shape, form, mountains, rivers, snakes, trees, etc.). It is said that one can acquire wisdom by watching nature. Perhaps there is much to learn if we simply watch how the grass grows. Water is a metaphor that is often used because it is shapeless and formless.

The third and final face of Tao is the *Te*. The Te is the Tao as it is manifested in the human spirit. This "Tao in myself" can be discovered through self-reflection and meditation. Together, these three faces of the Tao form the subject matter of Lao-Tzu's classic treatise, the *Tao-Te-Ching*.

* * *

Buddhism has also had a great influence in Japanese culture. However, politics has had an influence on the choice of religions. Relatively speaking, until fairly recently Japan has remained secluded from western society. Japan's society was really quite unlike its western invaders. Through contact with the west, it became apparent to the Japanese that they would have to change in order to compete or survive in the market. Historically, Germany has often been the center of financial, industrial, and technological successes, much in the same way that the United States is today. To take advantage of that industry and technology, Japan made alliances with Germany.

Japan needed to unite its people and make them more 'pure'. The Purist movement took Shinto and made it a state religion of Japan. Shinto was used to unify Japan and give its people a sense of importance. After World War II, however, the western world sought to break up the Japanese unity. The treaty of WW II stated that there would be no state religion allowed in Japan, so a separation of church and state was imposed. As we shall see, this is as impossible as ordering Israel to not have a state religion.

In Japan it is common to blend Shinto with Buddhism. When Japanese were surveyed about which religion they identified with, "93% answered Shinto, and 74% answered Buddhist."[13] We may say, "167%? That is impossible. There must be an error." No, there is no error. The spirituality of Shinto can co-exist with the practices of Buddhism.

The influence of Shinto is tightly woven with everyday comings and goings. Basic ideals include "primacy of feeling and intuition, inseparability of humanity from nature, and ethnocentrism."[14] Shrines are placed in locations of power, or

Kami (sacred presence). A typical day in the life of a Japanese person includes visiting a kami several times a day. What actually happens when the kami are visited is difficult to describe. There is no vocalization or idolization. For example, one does not sit before the kami and begin prayer with "Oh grateful kami..." Rather than vocalization, there is silence. This silence signifies the recognition of a sacred presence. Kami may be as abstract as a mountain (e.g. Mount Fuji). The majestic mountain demands a certain respect for the holiness of its nature. Kami are simply wherever there is considered to be a sacred presence.

The influence of Shinto on daily Japanese life becomes apparent when we visit the top of an office building in Tokyo and stumble upon a shrine. In the United States, the CEO of an important business is considered the most important person, demanding the utmost respect from all those below him or her. In Japan, above the CEO is the kami, for without the kami, we might say there would be no CEO! In many houses there is a shrine with a picture of the face of an ancestor. The members of the household visit the shrine daily. With this picture, the members of the present generation are reminded that they owe their very existence to a previous generation.

There are three levels to the Japanese self: the "social or 'interactional' self, the inner or 'reflective' self, and the 'boundless' chaotic self."[15] These levels give rise to a fascinating phenomenon called *migawari* (meaning 'surrogate'). By 'surrogate' is meant "allowing someone else to act in your place." This may seem odd or unacceptable to a western thinker, because westerners are unaccustomed to this tradition. Depending on the level of intimacy or authenticity that the situation demands, there often are situations when an exchange of identity with someone else is appropriate. For people raised with western values, some of the situations in which the

Japanese will accept a surrogate are indeed unthinkable. For example, if a dear relative of a westerner dies and a friend is unable to attend the funeral, a replacement for the would-be attender would probably be quite meaningless. However, in Japanese society it is not uncommon that someone else would go in place of the friend, with all the sincerity and sympathy that the original friend would have brought. This surrogate would offer all the comfort that the friend would liked to have offered. The surrogate is accepted as sincere and may be immensely appreciated.

A third party is often involved in arranging or proposing a marriage in Japan. In actuality, to the westerner, the Japanese method of 'courtship' may seem quite callous. The family is usually involved in the selection of a husband, and the process is much like the western idea of computer dating. A fiancee is valued for his financial success and future. The eligible partner is usually much older than his wife-to-be.

The wife is desired by the husband to produce children. Usually the husband's mother will move in with the wife to help her with the rearing of the children. This is often necessary, since in the highly competitive Japanese society, the husband must move from city to city to maintain his business position. Often the husband is available for little more than financial support. Taking a child out of school and moving around is frowned upon. As a result, the wife, mother, and child often live in separate apartments from the father. Life for the Japanese man consists of very hard work and long hours.

"Anti-egocentrism, loyalty for the sake of harmony, taking responsibility for others, and an emphasis on intimacy"[16] are valued traits in Japanese society and probably have much to do with Japan's success in the marketplace. For westerners, however, there is not much intimacy in the idea of spouses living apart from each other. In Japan, it is unlikely that one will prosper unless one is willing to adhere to these customs. Men make these sacrifices to remain competitive.

* * *

In discussion of a cross-cultural perspective, gender roles bear much importance in describing the self. The women's movements in western societies have spurred a new interest in the study of self in women. In Japan, the role of the mother is very influential. Women are extremely important in the rearing process. A woman is sought by a man when he is ready to support children. As a result, women in Japan rarely indulge in both a career and motherhood.

China generally is a patrilinear society. A boy is taught the importance of the role of being a son, then a father, and eventually a grandfather. A female child generally stays at home. Upon her marriage, a wife is removed from the home in which she was raised, and moves to live with her husband and his family. More often than not, this husband was not from the same village. In fact, there are instances when a woman may not ever see her family again. There is, again, a 'transfer' of identity upon marriage. In a sense, once she is married, a wife 'belongs' to someone else. A women actually has identity through someone else, be it her husband or son. For a Chinese woman, "her marriage and marriage of her son ... (render her) most vulnerable to suicide"[17] (because identity of self becomes confused). It is common for a mother to encourage her son to be dependent on her and to remain close to home.

In India as well, the father role is more influential. Women can have a career and be a mother. However, a woman's identity is still mainly defined through her relationships with others. An important factor when defining the self of a woman in India is her class of wealth. The four 'types' of women are "poor ... middle class ... upper middle class ... and rich."[18] The woman's class generally determines her education (many are illiterate) and status or position in society. Overall, gender issues in the study of the self are relatively new and the need for more research is pressing as it really seems as if we only see part of a biased view.

* * *

With growing technology and better communication, the east and the west have come into more and more contact with each other. Many Americans are finding job opportunities in Japan. Business people are often required to learn about the customs of other societies to facilitate business transactions. As a woman from the United States, I find it very difficult to define or pinpoint exactly where it is from in this world that I have inherited all my ideals. The world is truly evolving and becoming a 'melting pot'. Our relatively recent contact with this 'other world' has raised many new questions. When coffee is added to milk, we have a new product. With contact between the western societies and the eastern societies, we have developed a new world, with new combinations of people.

Western societies have much to benefit from this contact with the eastern philosophies. I believe that much western society lacks or overlooks the spirituality that is more common to everyday eastern philosophy. Perhaps westerners can learn from the Japanese. Perhaps it is important to take a moment or two of silence in the day to reflect, and realize that there is a reason why we become such things as a CEO of a company, or why nature is so grand and majestic. There are things that are beyond our understanding, and will probably always be. I believe that we must respect those things, for they are greater than us.

The Chinese also believe in collectivism, which of course is very much unlike western societal thought. Often westerners do not help one another, or take responsibility for each other's affairs. Individuality and autonomy are more valued in western societies.

From Buddhism, westerners can learn to respect other creatures of this world, through recognition that a life is a life, is a life. My personal experience is that the soul of other creatures is something that an individual has not experienced, so an individual cannot judge the soul of a 'lesser' creature. I anticipate that one day, when I am freed from the physical body to which I am in this life bound, I will be united with these other souls. Perhaps it is then that I will first begin to understand.

Perhaps other dog-owners can relate to this experience of mine. I have read somewhere that the I.Q. of the breed of dog that I own is about 40. A severely retarded human being may have an I.Q. of 40. However, we still make a very clear distinction between humans and animals. That is a notion that is harmonious to our egocentric ideals. I know that although limited, my dog has a vocabulary through which he and I can communicate. Should all animals not receive the same respect that any human is deserving of? We may believe that we are the highest form of the soul, but we should also recognize that life is given to any animal in much the same way it is given to us. Odd as it may seem, I often look into the eyes of my dog and see something much more than just 'Fido'. I see a soul with feelings, a soul that struggles for survival, for companionship, and for understanding of my words. If we consider reincarnation for a moment, then is it not possible to believe that his soul may one day take hold of human life?

Let us also recognize that there is much that western philosophy can offer to eastern philosophy. In the United States there is a "sense of individual rights and responsibilities, emphasis of integrity as based in fundamental principles of Law and morality, and encouragement of personal expression in a spirit of compromise."[19] Of course, many can argue that encouragement of personal expression may contribute to divorce. However, with the proper blend, we may achieve perfection.

Consider schooling in China, for example. Teaching there is based on an accepted 'party-line', and may even involve informants to keep the teacher 'in line' through censorship. In western society it is believed that it is a social responsibility to enforce academic freedom. In the United States censorship is deemed unjust. I truly believe that academic freedom is of great value. I am very fortunate to have the freedom to sit in a classroom and express my honest opinions of such things as politics, and to be able to expect an honest discussion from my teacher. I would certainly never want to trade that privilege or right for anything. Without academic freedom, how can one make clear, informed and educated decisions?

It requires effort to consider another philosophy without prejudice. It is my belief that the Japanese might find value in stressing more familial closeness. Perhaps financial success is not as important or vital as is customary in Japan. With compromise, maybe the father can spend more time with his wife and children, and receive satisfaction from his relationships with his family. In return, perhaps the mother can take time to pursue other endeavors. This is an idea that is even fairly new to western society. However, it is more and more common to find households in the United States in which both parents work, with both parents sharing the responsibility of the child rearing. This gives both males and females an opportunity to have many virtuous experiences they might otherwise have missed or gone without.

This brings me to an important point. As a woman, I know that I am very fortunate to be living in the United States. Although I am often angered by the discrimination I face on a day-to-day basis, I am fully aware that my level of autonomy would be shocking to most of the women from the eastern cultures we have discussed. It seems as if the eastern woman has yet to be 'liberated'. Of course, there remains the question as to whether she even desires to be or not. With this contact between cultures, at least she can become aware and choose of her own free will.

With more contact between western and eastern societies, much is beginning to change. Many young Japanese women are choosing to marry for Love. Women all over the world are seeking education and choosing careers. The standard of living has improved for many villages which before never had such things as running water.

With this fairly recent contact, there are bound to be conflicts and confrontations. Some ideas may be shocking. It is sometimes easier to accept what we have already accepted, and to believe that we have the best way. This initial prejudice will alter the perceptions we have of other philosophies. There is resistance from both sides to change. But neither side is entirely right, or wrong. Moderation is the key.

With much respect and effort, perhaps there can be a common ground from which we can all begin to build. I believe there is a common ground, as basic as life itself. If we have respect, then we can have understanding. With understanding, we can have sharing. With sharing, we will most definitely have improvement.

Notes

1. *Webster's New World Dictionary.*
2. *Self as Person in Asian Theory and Practice*, p. 215.
3. *Ibid*, p. 214.
4. *Ibid*, p. 279.
5. *Ibid*, p. 298.
6. *Ibid*, p. 298.
7. *Ibid*, p. 306.
8. *Ibid*, p. 178.
9. *Ibid*, p. 177.
10. *Ibid*, p. 183.
11. *Ibid*, p. 174.
12. *Ibid*, p. 175.
13. *Ibid*, p. 98.
14. *Ibid*, p. 98.
15. *Ibid*, p. 108.
16. *ibid*, p. 85.
17. *Ibid*, p. 176.
18. *Ibid*, p. 342.
19. *Ibid*, p. 85.

REFERENCES

Roger T. Ames, Wimal Dissanayake, and Thomas P. Kasulis, *Self as Person in Asian Theory and Practice*. Albany, New York: SUNY Press, 1994.

Victoria Neufeldt and Andrew N. Sparks, *Webster's New World Dictionary*. New York: Simon and Schuster, 1990.

QUALITY, LOVE, AND MADNESS: PIRSIG VERSUS PLATO

Kerri Nicholas
SUNY - Oneonta

Introduction

This paper deals with a comparison of the ideas presented in Plato's *Phaedrus* and Robert Pirsig's *Zen and the Art of Motorcycle Maintenance.* It looks at the journey of Robert Pirsig, his mind-altering search for Quality, and the way it leads him to Madness. Included also are differences and similarities between Pirsig's understanding of Love and Madness and Plato's treatment of those same topics in his dialogue, *Phaedrus.* The two works are tied together by their in-depth discussions concerning the relationships the main characters have toward each other and toward others who come into their lives.

Part One: Quality

What is Quality? Before I took a course in Metaphysics I probably would have answered that question without giving it a second thought. However, giving it a second thought opens up a whole new way to look at the question — which in turn gives you a third thought, a fourth thought, and so on. I have often heard people say to "make sure your reach does not exceed your grasp." I think that this statement should be a warning to anyone who attempts to define Quality. Every time I feel as though I have figured out just what is meant by the term "Quality", I notice that it has slipped just a little ways away from my definition. When I re-approach it, I encounter the same outcome.

Robert Pirsig hints at the problem of Quality very early in his book, *Zen and the Art of Motorcycle Maintenance*. He tells about experimenting with different hypotheses in his science courses when he first studied in college. This was the non-metaphysical stage of his encounter with Quality. He saw the problem arising, but did not explore it very deeply. He states that "the more you look, the more you see."[1] The more hypotheses he tested, the more hypotheses he generated. Pirsig explained: "instead of selecting one truth from the multitude you are increasing the multitude."[2]

Later in life, when faced with the seemingly innocent question of whether he was teaching Quality in his classes, Pirsig struggled to find a definition of Quality. The more he thought about the definition, the more options he found. This marked the beginning of the metaphysical stage of his Quality "problem". He began to think with greater intensity and ran into many perplexing obstacles. Each attempt to corner the truth made him see different aspects of the truth.

Pirsig examined the Subjective/Objective dichotomy. The Subjective side emphasized his own ideas of Quality while the Objective side focused on the world around him. He also looked critically at the Classical/Romantic split. The Classical view cuts things up and looks for Quality among, and in the relationships between, the parts. The Romantic view looks at the object as a whole, not cutting things apart with the intellectual scalpel. Eventually, Pirsig realized that maybe he should be looking for a trinity.

The trinity that Pirsig came up with describes Quality as an event which unites the Subjective and the Objective. "Quality" should really be a verb, even though it sounds like a noun. This realization came to him during the final stage of his search for the definition of Quality. He refers to this final stage as "the mystical stage." The mystical connection links Quality to both the Subjective and the Objective, but the Subjective also bridges itself with another Subjective idea. This, in turn, helps to bridge the difference between individuals. In a sense, we all become one in Quality.

Pirsig's mystical definition of Quality provides an example of the human need to bring closure to everything. Phaedrus[3] makes "everything" Quality. That seems to be his attempt to bring closure to the idea of Quality. But Quality is not a closed subject. It is always changing and it is different in the minds of each person.

Is it possible to teach Quality? Is it possible to teach the ability to apprehend Quality? Many people consider Quality to be subjective. If that is the case, Quality cannot really be taught. It can be learned in the sense that you can look at what others think is Quality and take some of their ideas to form your own characteristics of Quality. But you can not sit in a class and learn what Quality is. "Quality" is too broad of a term to be confined by the normal definitions given in a class.

Webster's *New World Dictionary* defines "Quality" as any of the features that make something what it is. When we strive to teach Quality, we use examples, not definitions. Everyone in our class was able to come up with an example of what they think of as Quality. But when it came down to an actual definition, most people were still stuck on the examples. Quality is not always how good something is, or how pleasing it is to us.

Everyone recognizes Quality somewhere in their life — whether it be in a piece of artwork in a museum or in a paper they write for their Metaphysics class. But trying to explain to someone how to recognize Quality is virtually impossible. Quality is subjective in the mind of the person examining things. It is almost as though everyone has an *a priori* sense of Quality. We look at things and our first reaction is usually one of like or dislike. We think to ourselves, "I don't like that; it is not of good Quality." But re-examining may allow us to realize that the subject does have a high Quality, even though it is not pleasing to us. We have a sense of Quality, as far as construction goes, in our mind already. We have a model of what is considered to be Quality.

So, maybe in a way, we *can* teach Quality to a certain extent. By learning what my parents thought was Quality, I in turn developed my own sense of Quality. It is my sense, even though I took ideas or forms from their opinions. It is not always easy to recognize Quality. Sometimes there is an underlying Quality that is not noticed on the surface level.

Quality plays a large role in our lives. One of its roles is to allow us a measure of comparison. Quality gives us a reference point from which we can see relationships between things that ordinarily would not be easily related to one another. The concept of Quality enriches our experiences of reality by giving us a larger scope from which to observe things. We do not have to always use the ideas of like and dislike: as I said before, Quality does not necessarily have to be pleasing to us. I will admit to the possibility of a high quality gun, even though I do not like guns.

"Quality" is an unbounded term that can be used in many different ways. To try and define it, you would find yourself up against diverse sets of competing definitions. So, the whole question of what Quality is cannot be answered by one person in one way. Quality is an ever-changing, dynamic idea that is a part of everyone's lives.

Part Two: Love and Madness

Often it is thought that love is a form of madness. This is true in the speech of Lysias, in Plato's dialogue *Phaedrus*. He looks upon the lover in an unfavorable way, describing lovers as "not sound, but sick; they know that they are incapable of good judgment, but cannot control themselves."[4] Most people upon the first encounter with this statement agree with it. I know that I did. We all know the feeling of not being completely sane when we first fall in love; that is part of its beauty. The romantic side of our personality falls right into this idea.

However, Lysias fails to follow the thought through to its proper conclusion. Love changes over time. The initial spark that you feel may be fanned and grow into the burning passion of eternal love, or it may be put out right away by not getting any attention. Lysias focuses on the here and now, not what may happen down the road. He also keeps his focus on this life in his speech. He focuses more on physical pleasure than on long-term happiness. He appeals to the opinions of society, rather than to select people from society.

When Socrates hears the speech of Lysias, he disagrees with both form and content. He makes that very clear to Phaedrus by saying that it was the young boy, not the speech by which he was enthralled. Then, to illustrate the weakness of Lysias' speech, Socrates himself makes a speech on the same subject as Lysias, arguing the same point as Lysias. In this context, he states that "a man in love is an utterly unprofitable guardian or associate."[5] He argues that you should stay away from the lover and put your interest instead with a non-lover. He tells of how love is madness and how madness should be avoided.

To atone for the sinful content of this speech in which he has argued alongside Lysias, Socrates then makes a second speech. Here he maintains that there is "no shame or reproach in madness" and that many ancestors "regarded madness under divine guidance."[6] In these statements, Socrates is arguing for the lover over the non-lover. He considers it more acceptable to have a lover than to be with a non-lover. He feels that not all madness is undesirable and that love is a desirable madness.

In his second speech, Socrates focuses on the immortal soul, rather than the present life. He looks at the lover as a source for eternal happiness, not just pleasure on the Earth. By being with a lover, you are attaining happiness, not just pleasure. You may also gain knowledge, friendship, and great companionship by having a lover. Socrates also looks to true wisdom in this speech. In order to have true wisdom, one cannot be clouded by temporary distractions in life. There must be some sort of focus and stability.

There is a poem by Kahlil Gibran that provides a perfect example of what Socrates is saying:

> At ebb tide I wrote
> A line upon the sand
> And gave it all my heart
> And all my soul.
> At flood tide I returned
> To read what I had inscribed
> And found my ignorance upon the shore.

True happiness cannot be found in impermanence. To use your affections on a non-lover is a waste of time. In a bad time the non-lover will not be there anymore — just like the inscription was gone when the author went back to it at flood tide. Ignorance is all that is left, and not a trace of what you had there before.

Socrates defines four divisions of madness. One of these four is love-madness, with the gods Eros and Aphrodite. This, he says, is declared to be the best form of madness. He asserts that his speech was "in honor of my master and yours, Phaedrus: Love, the guardian of beautiful boys."[7] According to this, there is no possible way to consider the non-lover as the better option. The gods will love, even if it leads to madness. Therefore the pious thing is not to simply seek pleasure from non-lovers, but to share life with a lover. "The lover's good will, discovered by this intimacy, astonishes the beloved who perceives that not all other men together, friends and relatives, can contribute even a tittle of affection in comparison with his inspired friend."[8] This shows how the lover touches the beloved in all aspects of life. The lover becomes inspired by the beloved. They share everything with one another, knowledge as well as companionship.

I think that Plato's views of Love and Madness, as told through this dialogue between Socrates and Phaedrus, is very interesting. It is easy to get caught up with Lysias' ideas that love is madness and that madness is bad. It is perhaps better and more accurate to regard a little madness as normal. Everyone is a little bit mad. Love is considered madness because the person who is in love does not have total control of what they do.

Robert Pirsig is a prime example of a person who lost control. Like the love discussed by Socrates and Phaedrus,

Pirsig's quest for understanding totally took over every detail of his life. He became so obsessed with finding out what Quality was, that he ended up losing touch with the very people who mattered most to him.

Perhaps if Pirsig had focused on love instead of Quality, he would not have had to look so far away. According to Plato, much knowledge comes through love. It is quite possible that if Pirsig had cultivated the relationship with his wife, his quest may not have taken him so far from home. Pirsig treated the time during which he looked for the definition of Quality as an entirely different lifetime. The old person was even given a different name: Phaedrus. Technically he was still in the same body, but his mental focus was markedly different.

Pirsig's love of knowledge and pursuit of Quality were driving him mad. Something about reading Plato's *Phaedrus* pushed him over the edge. This illustrates the fine line between madness and insanity. His pursuit of truth turned into complete obsession. He needed to know more, to find closure for his thoughts. He did not understand that love of knowledge is eternal; there is no closure. That is the Zen part: it is life; it is on-going; it is the future.

Love is a form of madness that varies in degree in each person's life. For Pirsig, the madness ultimately led to institutionalization and Electroshock Therapy ("Annihilation ECS").[9] For the average person the madness is not so extreme. Our madness usually only manifests itself in small ways — like causing us to put off our Metaphysics paper for a day! Whether the degree of madness is large or small, it can be noticed throughout the world around us.

NOTES

1. Pirsig, p. 101.
2. *Ibid.*
3. For reasons which will become apparent as we proceed, Robert Pirsig found it difficult to accept a portion of his life. To refer to the thoughts and perceptions of this period, he borrows the pseudonym *Phaedrus* from the Platonic dialogue of the same name.
4. Plato, p. 8.
5. *Ibid.*, p. 19.
6. *Ibid.*, p. 25.
7. *Ibid.*, p. 54.
8. *Ibid.*, p. 40.
9. Pirsig, p. 77.

REFERENCES

Pirsig, Robert. *Zen and the Art of Motorcycle Maintenance.* New York: Bantam Books, 1974.

Plato. *Phaedrus*. New York: Bobbs-Merrill, 1956.

Historical Reflections

Nietzsche's Appropriative Representation *or* Is the Overman a Hermaphrodite?

John D. Devine
Alfred University

Consciously and unconsciously, the question of how to read Nietzsche has been addressed for a century. The recent attention paid to Nietzsche's rhetorical and interpretive theories has given the enterprise new life. As Nietzsche is increasingly examined as a contemporary philosopher — by contemporary philosophers — it seems we are allowing Nietzsche to answer this question himself. In *Nietzsche's Voice*, Henry Staten performs what he terms a "pyschodialectical" reading of Nietzsche, justifying his interpretation with Nietzsche's own writings:

> It is Nietzsche himself who teaches us to look for the influence on his writing, as on that of any philosophy, of instinct, drive and desire.[1]
>
> ...we ask how Nietzsche's drives secretly guide his conscious thinking into certain channels.[2]

However, in any reading infused with a psychoanalytic gestalt there are recognizable dangers. Nietzsche warns us against "pot peeking" by which we might

> reduce the whole author's effort to nothing; so that they deservedly gain, not a philosophic outlook or instruction, but — at best, or at worst — nothing more than the satisfaction of vulgar curiosity.[3]

It there is anything we might call Sigmund Freud, it is a voyeur. Staten avoids this pitfall in his refusal to identify particular moods or moments of Nietzsche's life as essential in the way a traditional psychoanalytic method might. He advises instead that we look to more general libidinal drives.

The issue of voyeurism — indeed the commission of voyeurism — opens the door (or perhaps it peers in the keyhole) to the intrigue of sexuality. The marked attention given to sexuality and its relationship to writing for Nietzsche runs dangerously close to perpetrating that other great Freudian error: the essentialization of all activity as sexual. Nonetheless, and taking Staten's advice to heart, I will succumb to this danger's calling. If I must request Nietzsche's approval to run this course, I will take this passage from *Beyond Good and Evil* as his proximal response:

> The degree and kind of a person's sexuality reach up into the ultimate pinnacle of his spirit.[4]

* * *

When Zarathustra first presents himself to the people his speech is fiery and fervent. His words are rhythmic, frenzied, and he stands, shouts, waving his arms and his thoughts. For all of this the crowd is still disinterested. Their attention, instead, is focused overhead where another play is being acted out. The tightrope walker mesmerizes the crowd — and it is quite a show they get! As the acrobat is making his careful steps toward his goal another figure leaps onto the rope. It is the jester, and he mocks the performer; laughing as he leaps *over* him, laughing as he sends the tightrope walker to his death.

Thus we have *Zarathustra*'s first image of the overman. The agile jester has managed to jump *over* the tightrope walker, to go beyond his lame attempt to cross the rope "between beast and overman."[5] Zarathustra encounters the jester later that evening by the gates of the city. "Verily," says the jester, "you talked like a jester today."[6] Zarathustra, for all his failings, at least *talked* like a jester. It seems, then, that the style in which Zarathustra speaks (and also, then, Nietzsche's style) is a significant clue to understanding the overman[7].

In Nietzsche's lectures on ancient rhetoric there is at least one passage which seems appropriate to an analysis of Zarathustra's well adorned language:

> Embellishment, thus, requires that one carry over appropriateness into a higher sphere of the laws of beauty; it is a transfiguration of what is typical, first, through the elimination of the less noble in what is typical, and then, through the enhancement of the noble and beautiful, which are important traits of what is typical. Embellishment is a higher nature, in contrast to common naturalness; reproduction, in contrast to imitation and mimicry.[8]

The entire passage resonates of the overman. The sexuality of the writing enters here in two ways. First in the call for reproduction; reproduction and rebirth are always the generation of the overman. Secondly, the issue of appropriateness, the appropriateness of a style of speech to the overman, gives itself over to further sexual manipulation.

Appropriateness is a sense of belonging, and can be seen here as part of what Derrida calls "a process of propriation".[9] Propriation is Derrida's term for any action of giving/taking, and is the keystone to Nietzsche's analysis of the sexes. Derrida writes:

> Either, at times, woman is woman *because she gives* herself, while man for his part takes, possesses, indeed takes possession. Or else, at other times, she is woman because she is in fact *giving herself for*, is simulating, and

> consequently assuring the positive mastery of her own self.[10]

Throughout *Spurs* Derrida suggests that Nietzsche's style is a woman. Nietzsche, his intriguing body of work, seduces from a distance. For Derrida, woman represents Truth while the marriage contract acts as the paradigm for the promise of Truth. The marriage to Truth is never consummated, the textual woman never penetrated; the hymen is never broken.

In Nietzsche's lectures on rhetoric he says that appropriateness aims at a moral effect. Appropriateness holds a moral sway over an audience by instilling them with a sense of the author's sincerity. Keeping in mind the contrast between moral sway and Derrida's rather immoral seduction, we could imagine that Zarathustra's sincere and grandiose style would carry with it the surfeit of truth.

If writing is appropriate to an audience, and is appropriated by an audience, then the act of writing becomes an act of giving. That the overman should involve himself in an act of giving is certainly not surprising, but as an act of propriation it might call into question the overman's masculinity. Nietzsche writes:

> But all embellishment must be masculinely powerful and dignified, *sanctus* [pure], free from effeminate frivolity and false cosmetic.[11]

There is a possibility of reconciliation here. The second type of giving, the *giving for*, puts the woman of style in a position to take possession of herself; thus she also takes the masculine position. "Male and female change places. They exchange masks *ad infinitum*"[12]. The *giving for* also reveals how appropriateness holds moral sway over an audience — it is the veiled ability of a woman to seize the position of power. This appropriation is done without the knowledge of the other, partner, audience; the womanly inclinations toward self possession through the (sexual) act (of writing) are veiled in masculinity. Nietzsche continues the discussion of masculinity/effeminacy: "Here, though, the boundary between vice and virtue is very narrow."[13] Had Nietzsche revealed his womanly desires, the moral sway he held would have been lost.

The presence of woman — truth — for Derrida is always marked by the frustration of the unbroken hymen. In *Spurs* the unbroken hymen will inevitably cause the *l'erection tombe*. This expression has two possible translations: either "the erection falls" or "the erection tomb."[14] The motif of simulation, sexuality and *l'erection tombe* makes a particular tale of Dionysus an irresistible addition to this discussion. In it, Dionysus seeks passage to Hades to bargain for his mother's life.

> He went by way of Lake Lerna, a bottomless lake, which was said to offer the quickest access to Hades. But since he did not know the way, Dionysus had to make enquiries from a man named Prosymnus (or Polymnus), who asked certain favors as a reward, to be paid on Dionysus' way back. The god was unable to pay him these favors when he returned, for Prosymnus had died meanwhile; so Dionysus did his best to keep his promise by fashioning a stick into the appropriate phallic shape and planting it in Prosymnus' tomb.[15]

The tale of Prosymnus' *l'erection tombe* gives us a different twist on the expression. It is first important to note the absence of any hymen in this presumed act of simulation. It is this absence which guarantees the impossibility of Truth. The hymen is, in the case of Nietzsche, inappropriate to the act because it represents the very possibility of Truth, a possibility the overman must reject.

This might seem to suggest that it is, in fact, a homosexual act which is the generation of the overman. On the very surface there are serious questions as to this conclusion's legitimacy — the homosexual act cannot lead to procreation. It is reproduction which is the prime activity of the overman.

The homosexual act — the act of two men — is a misunderstanding. It is a misunderstanding which, in part, Derrida has lead us into: "the man, for his part, takes, possesses, indeed takes possession."[16]. It is this last formulation which gives us the homosexual; the act of propriation reiterated. It is the man taking the masculine, a man taking a man. On this model the act of the woman, in her *giving for*, seizes first herself and then the masculine principle.

This scheme of double proprietivity inevitably falls into one of simultaneous double representation in each sexual scenario. The woman of style expropriates masculinity, and in doing so she also takes herself. When thought of as an act of writing, an audience is introduced which reduces the act from propriation to representation. Woman — Truth — is only represented and promised. This makes the very action of *giving for* most significantly an exercise in simulation. Thus in the *giving for,* in writing for an audience, we also have a case of self deferred. And in Dionysus' tale there seems to be an instance of self, or presence, deferred — and also an instance of woman deferred and represented.

The error here, the error in a motif of double propriation/representation, is in considering the homosexual act one where woman is deferred. The homosexual act is not simulation; it is not symbolic replacement. It only appears symbolic from a heterocentric perspective in which the hymen is eschatologically fundamental, and therefore the defining characteristic of the (sexual) act (of writing). Double propriation does not occur in the overman's writing, in *giving for*, and its proof is the very ability of a male to act as woman. The homosexual act demonstrates that there is no necessary relationship between gender and position, no appropriate propriation.

The impossibility of double propriation would finally open the possibility of breaking Derrida's hymen. In the magician's song, or *The Song of Melancholy*, Nietzsche discusses the relationship to truth as a kind of courtship:

> "Suitor of truth?" they mocked me; "you?"
> No! Only Poet!
> An animal, cunning, preying, prowling,
> That must lie,
> That must knowingly, willingly lie:
> Lusting for prey,
> Colorfully masked,
> A mask for itself,
> Prey for itself—
> *This*, the suitor of truth?
> No! Only Fool! Only poet!
> Only speaking colorfully,
> Only screaming colorfully out of fools' masks,
> Climbing around on mendacious word bridges,
> On colorful rainbows,
> Between false heavens
> and false earths,
> Roaming, hovering—
> *Only* fool! *Only* poet![17]

This should not be taken as a description of Nietzsche's, or Zarathustra's relationship with truth. The conscientious man objects to the song:

> ... beware when such as you start making speeches and fuss about truth! Woe unto all free spirits who do not watch out against such magicians![18]

Lest for that woeful demon — time — the song would seem to satirize Derrida's entire position. In *On the Poet*, Nietzsche makes similar allusions, claiming that the poet lies to explore the limit of skepticism, deride logic and guarantee the prosperity of "magicians" and their "intimation"[19]. In *Nietzsche on Truth and Philosophy*, Maudemarie Clark argues that Nietzsche's perspective does not exclude logic or truth, only a metaphysical version of either.[20] The double proprietivity entangles itself with a metaphysical position by assuming that there are not only properties (eg. masculine, feminine, true, false), but also that these properties need to have a proper place and position.

The overman's (sexual) act (of writing) must be one which can be performed within one self. This should not, however, lead us into an individualistic reading of Nietzsche. The Derridian heterocentric reading is flawed because its focus is on difference. In such a reading the other, partner's, audience's other*ness* is the most important feature of the relationship. The conscientious man continues his indictment of the magician: "You praise me by distinguishing me from yourself"[21].

From this perspective the act of writing is purely a consummation of self. The act of the overman, after all, is an act of self-overcoming. As such, any sexual metaphors for the act of writing are only tropes for the relationship of writer to writing. The writer breaks the hymen and finds his own truth. To this we can only bear posthumous witness, only have a stick in the mud. Here Dionysus' act is only representation, and further it gives the appearance of necrophilia. And, as such, we might come to see the heterocentric reading as always being somewhat necrophilistic, always obsessed with penetrating a dead body of work. Writing cannot be purely individualistic without sucking every bit of life from it. An individualistic, self-consummation model of self-overcoming turns a blind eye to all of Nietzsche's giving, to the overflowing cup of Zarathustra.

Neither should the overman's act of writing, though it is performed by oneself, be construed as a futile exercise in masturbation. Masturbation is nothing if not a manifest lack of creativity.

The procreative act is a consummation of and with self which takes place in the *giving for*, the giving–taking, which is the union of the male and female. The single organism which can engage in the procreative act can only be a hermaphrodite. Male and female do not simply exchange masks, they do so *ad infinitum*; and if this is truly *ad infinitum* exchange then exchange no longer takes place. The two have merged into one. The union of male and female in one ego is a common feature of Nietzsche's philosophy. It is the union of the feminine "life" with the masculine "wisdom" which Nietzsche fantasizes about in *Zarathustra*. Or it is the admixture of the masculine virility and the gift-giving virtue, which is most often discussed using vessels — cups, bowls — always symbols of woman. In any case, it is a balance between the masculine and the feminine position.

In all fairness to Derrida, the word "hermaphroditic" does at least appear in *Spurs,* and he certainly makes allusions to homosexuality. But in failing to address it as an important issue it becomes only a spurring suggestion and a bit of tongue in cheek humor.[22] If Nietzsche is sincere when he writes that it is the "degree and kind of a person's sexuality"[23] which pervades his spirit, the question of Friedrich Nietzsche's own sexuality must be seriously addressed if sexuality is addressed at all.

The hermaphrodite has no predefined sexual orientation, therefore no obsession with woman or truth. The very issue of gender is irrelevant for hermaphrodites because the hermaphrodite escapes any definite classification.[24] It is here that I can end my brush with danger, particularly the brush of a Freudian reading of Nietzsche. If gender is irrelevant for the over-man/hermaphrodite, the sexual readings of writing amount to no more than a playful trope, and is no less important for it.

If there still does not seem to be an escape from individualism and simulation here, it is because hermaphroditism is being considered at a distance, which is still the mark of a heterocentric reading. This heterocentric obsession with difference corresponds to an equally perverse homocentric obsession with sameness. A homocentric reading would be a complete identification with the text and it's contents.[25] If we can come to see the heterocentric and the homocentric as sharing the common error of imbalance (the error of the tightrope walker) we might become hermaphroditic readers. Not unlike methods of radical interpretation, a hermaphroditic reading would not be a search for Truth or its denial. It goes further than radical interpretation (Nietzsche, it seems, would always like us to go further) in reading for the act, reading for the life-affirming pleasure it gives. If the reader finds truth, the act was creative; and it seems the same must hold for finding falsehood. It is a reading, then, which not only attempts to penetrate the text, the corpus of Nietzsche's work, but allows that it should also penetrate you.

For the Dionysian writer, for the presumed homosexual, (but perhaps not for the homosexual writer) the hymen, the possibility of truth, is *not* absent; it is *irrelevant*. The hymen is evidence of the lack of consummation — the failure to keep a very particular promise. Prosymnus' *l'erection tombe* is a very different sort of promise, and is one which can be kept. The wooden phallus in the mud (Nietzsche's body of work) — its hardness, virility and penetration — should attest to this, and should lead us toward a new *l'erection tombe*. The promise here is of a life-affirming activity, which however ironically performed with the dead, still leads to consummation. Nietzsche gives us the possibility of a world which simply has sexuality and writing, which implores us to explore, to read, and moreover to *live* through these activities. In such a world the marriage contract will simply cease to exist.

NOTES

1. Henry Staten, *Nietzsche's Voice*, 9.
2. *Ibid.*, 10.
3. Friedrich Nietzsche, "Mixed Opinions and Maxims" in *Portable Nietzsche*, 65.
4. Friedrich Nietzsche, "Beyond Good and Evil" in *Portable Nietzsche*, 444.
5. Friedrich Nietzsche, "Thus Spoke Zarathustra" in *Portable Nietzsche*, 126.
6. *Ibid.*, 133.
7. Henry Staten gives a reasonable justification of not distinguishing "Nietzsche" from "Zarathustra" in the introduction to *Nietzsche's Voice*. By the same token I see no way to differentiate the "Dionysian" from the "overman", as they were the respective goal of each.
8. Friedrich Nietzsche, "Lectures on Ancient Rhetoric" in *Friedrich Nietzsche on Rhetoric and Language*, 43.
9. Jacques Derrida, *Spurs*, 109.
10. *Ibid.*
11. Friedrich Nietzsche, "Lectures on Ancient Rhetoric", in *Friedrich Nietzsche on Rhetoric and Language*, 41.
12. Jacques Derrida, *Spurs*, 110.
13. Friedrich Nietzsche, "Lectures on Ancient Rhetoric", in *Friedrich Nietzsche on Rhetoric and Language*, 41.
14. Barbara Harlow, trans., *Spurs* by Jacques Derrida, 153.
15. Pierre Grimal, *The Dictionary of Classical Mythology*, 410.
16. Jacques Derrida, *Spurs*, 109.

17. Friedrich Nietzsche, "Thus Spoke Zarathustra", in *Portable Nietzsche*, 410.

18. *Ibid.*, 413.

19. Friedrich Nietzsche, "Lectures on Ancient Rhetoric", in *Friedrich Nietzsche on Rhetoric and Language,* 243.

20. Maudemarie Clark, *Nietzsche on Truth and Philosophy.*

21. Friedrich Nietzsche, "Thus Spoke Zarathustra" in *Portable Nietzsche,* 413.

22. It might also be said in Derrida's defense that *Spurs* is not so much concerned with Nietzsche's philosophy as it with his style. Derrida, though, weaves the two into one analysis (if Derrida ever does only *one* analysis) which is, in my view, incompatible with the tenets of Nietzsche's philosophy.

23. Friedrich Nietzsche, "Beyond Good and Evil," in *Portable Nietzsche*, 444.

24. Here it might seem I am making rather bold statements flying in the face of the overwhelming opinion that Nietzsche is hopelessly misogynistic. This disparity forces me to turn the psychodialectic onto myself. I feel profoundly opposed to anything which smacks of misogyny, and I will recognize it's potential to color my reading. It must be admitted that the worship of hermaphrodites does not categorically exclude the devaluation of females, and it certainly did not for the ancient Greeks. Nietzsche's position could run close to the Greek here, where sexuality is at it's highest form in the homosexual encounter, and a union with woman is only by necessity. I am inclined to take a more benevolent reading, judging by the abundance of feminine symbolism, the characterization of life as a woman, and, as Derrida points out, his tendency to make an equation between the Jews and women. His hatred of anti–semites was partially based in the anti–semites' propensity to force semitic people into the very positions they scorned, the positions they saw as fundamentally Jewish. My own feelings on the devaluation of women run in many of the same directions.

25. A dramatic example of a homocentric reading might be given in Ray Bradbury's *Fahrenheit 451*. This occurred to me while reading Joshua Remy's "What Guides the Fool?". Joshua writes: "The people in *Fahrenheit 451* start communes all over the world where each person becomes a book; memorizing a whole book and burning the book..." XXXIV.

References

Clark, Maudemarie. *Nietzsche on Truth and Philosophy*. Cambridge: Cambridge University Press, 1990.

Derrida, Jacques. *Spurs*. Barbara Harlow (translator). Chicago: University of Chicago Press, 1979.

Dibrell, William. "The Dionysian Significance of the Eternal Return." *Historical Reflections/Reflexions Historiques,* Vol 21, No. 3, forthcoming.

Grimal, Pierre. *Dictionary of Classical Mythology*. A.R. Maxwell–Hyslop (translator). New York: Blackwell, 1985.

Nietzsche, Friedrich. *Friedrich Nietzsche on Rhetoric and Language*. Edited and translated by Sander L. Gilman, Carole Blair and David J. Parent. New York: Oxford University Press, 1989

Nietzsche, Friedrich. *The Portable Nietzsche*. Selected and translated by Walter Kaufmann. New York: Penguin Books, 1982.

Otto, Walter F. *Dionysus, Myth and Cult*. Robert B. Palmer (translator). Dallas: Spring Publications, 1986.

Remy, Joshua. "What Guides the Fool?"

Rorty, Richard. *Contingency, Irony, and Solidarity*. Cambridge: Cambridge University Press, 1989.

Staten, Henry. *Nietzsche's Voice*. Ithaca: Cornell University Press, 1990.

THE IMPOSSIBILITIES, IRRATIONALITY, AND CONTRADICTIONS OF IMMANUEL KANT'S ETHICAL THEORIES

David Schaaf
SUNY - Oneonta

Immanuel Kant was a brilliant philosopher, but his analysis of ethics was flawed in several fundamental ways. This paper examines his concept of a categorical imperative as well as his view concerning what does and does not qualify as moral behavior. Discussion of the views of John Stuart Mill and William David Ross adds to the refutation of Kant's ethical theories and suggests a direction for a reasonable, rational ethic.

* * *

Kant based his discussion of ethical theories on the concept of a good will. He argued that that and that alone is good in and of itself: "Nothing in the world, indeed nothing even beyond the world, can possibly be conceived which could be called good without qualification except a good will."[1] Kant claimed that it is the function of reason to produce a good will and guide it to commit morally right actions: "... reason's proper function must be to produce a will good in itself and not one good merely as a means, for to the former reason is absolutely essential."[2]

For an action to be morally right, it must fulfill the requirements of Kant's categorical imperative. This principle defines a moral law as one that is universally held by all people and universally adhered to in all circumstances and situations, without exception: "Act only according to that maxim by which you can at the same time will that it should become a universal law."[3]

Kant argued that we have a duty to follow the categorical imperative and do what is morally right. However, Kant held that an action is not morally right if you do it for the purpose of obtaining a particular result or if you act merely according to duty (without proper commitment and attitude). An action is deemed to be morally right only if the agent commits the action from duty, believes it to be morally right, and does so out of respect for moral law, without any result in mind. Kant explains:

> Duty is the necessity of acting from respect for the law... Now an action done from duty must wholly exclude the influence of inclination, and with it every object of the will, so that nothing remains which can determine the will except objectively the law, and subjectively pure respect for this practical law, and consequently the maxim that I should follow this law even to the thwarting of all my inclinations... Thus the moral worth of an action does not lie in the effect expected from it, nor in any principle of action which requires to borrow its motive from this expected effect... The preeminent good which we call moral can therefore consist in nothing else than the conception of law in itself, which certainly is only possible in a rational being, in so far as this conception, and not the expected effect, determines the will.[4]

Additionally, Kant believed that what is morally right must be held *a priori*, not based on experience or *a posteriori* facts. Any end based on *a posteriori* facts is a conditional end, subject to change, not absolute, and therefore not universal.

* * *

My first point of disagreement concerns Kant's categorical imperative. As said before, the categorical imperative requires a moral law to be universally accepted by all people and universally adhered to in all situations and circumstances, without exception. While the idea has some theoretical merit, application would be impractical at best.

Consider, for example, the idea of truth-telling. Avoiding conscious fabrication and/or misrepresentation of the truth is generally and justifiably considered a morally correct course of behavior. Hypothetically speaking, suppose this principle is transformed into a categorical imperative. In addition, assume that your best friend, who you know for a fact to be innocent of any and all crimes, is staying in your home. Suppose a man comes to your door, asking for your friend with the clear, announced intention of killing him. It seems obvious that the correct moral response involves telling the would-be killer that you do not know where your friend's whereabouts. In fact, to truthfully reveal the location of your friend, who you know for a fact to be innocent of any wrongdoing, is undoubtedly cruel, vicious, and immoral. However, under Kant's concept of a categorical imperative, lying would be immoral — even in a situation such as this.

In a second example, consider "Thou Shall Not Kill", one of God's Ten Commandments (per Judaism, Christianity, and Islam). Certainly, the prohibition against killing is a valuable moral principle; yet even this allows of exceptions. For instance, in a time of war, you are expected to attack and kill your enemy. Or in a matter of self-defense, in which you are an innocent person with your life unjustly threatened by another person, it is not immoral to kill your attacker if that is required to protect your own life. But if the moral principle is interpreted as an inflexible, universal, exceptionless law (per Kant's categorical imperative), fighting for your country or to protect your own life would be judged an immoral course of behavior.

Examples such as these help to prove that it is, at least from a practical perspective, impossible to apply a law to all situations at all times without exceptions. In some cases, it may actually be immoral to do so.

* * *

There may be those who wish to respond that the examples I have given prove only that the aforementioned maxims are not universal. Perhaps surprisingly, this type of argumentation serves to further undermine the credibility of Kant's concept of the categorical imperative. If you agree that the maxims are not universal and if, like Kant, you use the categorical imperative as a defining standard of that which is moral, it follows that you must reject not only the maxims but any behavior based on those maxims as non-moral. Surely, no one in their right mind will embrace the conclusion that the Biblical prohibition against killing is non-moral. The conclusion is too strong, and the problems lies not in the prohibition, but in the standard by which it is judged.

If "Thou shalt not kill" admits of exceptions, how much more so must this be true of rules governing lesser transgressions? The categorical imperative can never be applied without doing violence to the principles themselves, treating moral guidelines as though they were exceptionless laws. As such, the categorical imperative is an unrealistic and useless impossibility. As John Stuart Mill explained,

> It is not the fault of any creed, but of the complicated nature of human affairs, that rules of conduct cannot be so framed as to require no exceptions, and that hardly any kind of action can safely be laid down as either always obliga-

> tory or always condemnable. There is no ethical creed which does not temper the rigidity of its laws, by giving a certain latitude, under the moral responsibility of the agent, for accommodations to peculiarities of circumstances. [5]

* * *

Kant's categorical imperative gives rise to a serious contradiction, but it is not a contradiction contained in any of his texts or the manner in which he stated his ethical theories. The contradiction arises instead from the attempted application of his concept to the real world. Drawing on the work of Kant, William David Ross favored a deontological approach to ethics. But unlike Kant, he did not insist that meant applying exceptionless principles to real life situations. To bridge the distance between deontological principles and actual practice, Ross developed a theory of *prima facie* obligations.

A *prima facie* obligation is a type of ideal: in an uncomplicated (typically unrealistic) situation in which there are no other obligations, it provides complete, binding moral guidance. In practice, however, a *prima facie* obligation is not absolute. The particular circumstances in which humans find themselves are often far messier than the ideals on which these principles are based. Analysis of a complex situation may disclose several, potentially competing, *prima facie* obligations.

To accommodate the complexity of the situations with which we may be forced to deal, Ross introduced the concept of "actual obligation." Determining our actual obligation requires both moral sensitivity and reasoning concerning anticipated consequences. The objective is to aim for the "greatest" balance of right over wrong in that particular circumstance. In effect, Ross transformed the Kantian ideal into a type of utilitarian calculus, in which we aim for the greatest balance of right over wrong instead of the greatest amount of happiness.

* * *

As indicated previously, Kant does not consider an action to be morally right unless the agent acts from duty, believes the action to be morally right, and does so out of respect for moral law, without any result in mind. Like the concept of the categorical imperative, it is a standard which is problematic at best. Surely any law — whether it be formal or informal, legal or personal — is created with an intended result or objective in mind. If the desired behavior were automatic, a law would not be needed. Thus, by committing himself to acting in accordance with moral law, Kant automatically commits himself to acting in accordance with an intended result.

I readily concede that Kant is searching for a supreme principle of morality, looking for moral laws based upon *a priori* reasoning rather than *a posteriori* facts. However, this does not negate the empirical feature of law indicated above. Whether we are dealing with *a priori* reasoning or *a posteriori* facts, laws are created, held, and judged in terms of how well they promote a particular result or objective.

* * *

To further illustrate the irrationality of Kant's ethical theories, suppose there are two friends: Jack and John. Suppose that Jack has a very attractive girlfriend, Jill. Suppose further that John is single and unattached. Jill secretly asks John to have sex with her. John, seeing how attractive Jill is, desires to do so. However, John, mindful of his friendship with Jack, turns Jill down.

According to Kant, because John desires sex with Jill, his action has no moral worth. Kant explains, "Now an action done from duty must wholly exclude the influence of inclination."[6] While we might have preferred John not to have been tempted at all, surely the Kantian judgment is too harsh. John honored his friendship above sexual gratification, resisting the opportunity for a quick indulgence with an attractive girl. Even if he does not qualify for sainthood, John surely deserves some credit.

Kant's requirements for what determines a moral action are too rigid. In some cases, such as this one, they are totally out of touch with what morality really is. John's desire does not strip his action of moral value. In fact, it can even be argued that the desire makes his action more moral: the desire to have sex with Jill complicates the situation, makes it more difficult for John to ascertain the correct course of action, and increases considerably the moral effort he must muster in order to "do the right thing." It is only by resisting temptation that John is able to do what he knows to be morally correct.

Once again, searching for an ally in my disagreement with Kant, I find myself drawn to the writings of John Stuart Mill. In his essay *Utilitarianism*, Mill states,

> no system of ethics requires that the sole motive of all we do shall be a feeling of duty; on the contrary, ninety-nine hundredths of all our actions are done from other motives, and rightly done so... He who saves a fellow creature from drowning does what is morally right, whether his motive be duty, or the hope of being paid for his trouble.[7]

An ethical action is ethical in and of itself at all times, regardless of the motivation behind it. The morality of an action cannot be taken away simply due to one's motivation for committing the act.

NOTES

1. Kant, p. 184.
2. *Ibid.*, p. 184.
3. *Ibid.*, p. 198.
4. *A History of Western Philosophy*, pp. 72-73.
5. Mill, p. 5.
6. Kant, *Foundations on the Metaphysics of Morals*.
7. Mill, *Utilitarianism*.

REFERENCES

A History of Western Philosophy: Kant to Wittgenstein and Sartre (second edition). New York: Harcourt, Brace, and World, Inc., 1952.

Beauchamp, Thomas L. *Philosophical Ethics: An Introduction to Moral Philosophy* (second edition). New York: McGraw-Hill, 1991.

Immanuel Kant, *Foundations on the Metaphysics of Morals*, in *Ethics: Selections from Classical and Contemporary Writers* (Oliver A. Johnson, editor). Harcourt Brace College Publishers, pp. 183-207.

Mill, John Stuart. *Utilitarianism* (Oskar Piest, editor). Indianapolis: Bobbs-Merrill Company, 1957.

Sahakian, William S. *Outline-History of Philosophy*. New York: Barnes and Noble, 1968.

DESCARTES AND NIETZSCHE

Tatiana Zelikina
Moscow State University

The history of philosophy contains many revolutions. In a certain sense, every distinguished philosopher was himself a revolution: every one of them had his own system that, despite its similarity to others was still, as a whole, unique. The philosophic tradition is very rich, yet at different times the great philosophers tend to see it in different ways: some object to the tradition for the sake of building a new one, some follow it to a certain extent, and some ignore it. In other words, every philosopher sees the former tradition in a particular way. Even if they *seem* not to, that itself *is* a position in the history. The two revolutions in the philosophic tradition (Descartes and Nietzsche) discussed here are essentially different. They show (a) two kinds of responses to the history of thought, (b) what it is like to start a new theory, and (c) two kinds of views on philosophy as it was "before oneself" and as it is "related to oneself."

What is the point of Nietzsche calling his book 'On the Genealogy of Morals' a "polemic"?

A polemic presupposes at least two opinions that are confronting with one another, it is not a monologue or a reflection on a certain point, it rather a discussion and quite a challenging one. Furthermore, a polemical discussion is meant to discover a true way of *action* rather than thinking. It is not a mere speculation on some more or less relevant topic, but rather a current argument concerning further activity.

The apparent difference between a discussion and a polemic is the following: there might be no winner in a discussion, both sides might be content with what they hold even after the argument; in a polemic, on the other hand, there must be a winner — the one whose argument is stronger, the one that from now on would direct the thought and action.

These statements are fully applicable to Nietzsche's book, and even further, to his philosophy. Nietzsche's works have a new style, a new form, because they had (in his time) a new purpose in philosophy. Nietzsche is no longer concerned with the philosophical tradition in the sense that it might be useful for the further generations to correct their views or oppose them to the former ones. Nietzsche's view on tradition is of a different sort: he does not merely reject it (he often does not even use a reasonable method of opposing the former philosophy), he recognizes it to be of no use whatsoever. Nietzsche even goes beyond that, for it is not the former philosophy that he dislikes or rejects, it is the whole European anthropological view of a human being. Nietzsche's philosophy itself is more of a world view and this view clearly conflicts with the whole of European historical development.

The time that Nietzsche wrote his book was perfect for this very type of ideas. Nietzsche does not speak for himself only, but expresses a whole new world view that appears to have been popular with the younger generation.

Nietzsche suspends the judgment on all the former values and "on the value of these values"; he starts with the *critique*, and builds his whole system on it. Nietzsche might be a totally new type of philosopher, and it might be questionable as to whether or not he actually is a philosopher. The answer might be both positive and negative:

1. Nietzsche is not a philosopher if what we have in mind is the old conception of philosophy: Nietzsche does not think and write in terms of ontology, epistemology, etc.

2. Nietzsche is an outstanding philosopher and thinker of his time: he himself is a model of his time, he himself symbolizes the new philosophy and the new school of thought that was about to rise.

Both views on Nietzsche's thought are justified, yet one can no longer philosophize in terms of Hegel's dialectic. The twentieth century had to accept the new notion of philosophy in order to save it at all, and that is why Nietzsche's thought is a philosophical one — yet its form and content are somewhat unusual.

Had Nietzsche written a classical book in the manner of German thought, his book would have been placed on the shelf beside the rest of them as another (perhaps even a good) attempt to clarify the nature of reality. Nietzsche, however, did not want that to happen. He is challenging nothing less than the European Culture and Moral Tradition itself; he assumes that the time has come for a new type of man to arise, the superman that will be a master of himself, of his will. For Nietzsche, God is dead and the man of the present (that is, of Nietzsche's time) is not the type of man that is supposed to leave when God is dead; there has to be a new human being that *is* a God to himself. (Nietzsche's famous statement about the dead God is itself challenging: he does not say that 'there is no God'. Instead, Nietzsche makes God personal by saying that he is dead.

What is the difference between 'Genealogy' and 'History'?

The main difference between these two is in the direction that they have: history 'goes' forward, while genealogy is meant to investigate the past the other way around, i.e. it goes deeper and deeper in search of origins. Thus, in history the *causal* connection plays an important role, for it is mostly due to the causal connection that historical events occur. The genealogy does not deal with cause and effect; it seeks final explanations, the origins of the object that is under consideration.

In Nietzsche's book, though, these two are drawn together, for he believes that the origin might be found through the investigation of history as it actually occurred. The history of morals may show the functions (and the dysfunctions), the strong and weak points not with respect to the present society, but with respect to the origin functions and initial purposes (if there were such). If there were none, the history would help us to see why we had the morals we did and why we still have them now. In short it all might be summarized in the following scheme:

the origin ---- the history ---- morals as we
of morals   of morals   have them now

In this scheme, as Nietzsche assumes, the history of morals has made the original function/act more obscure to us. We have taken morals in a different way; yet it is necessary to know the history, for that is the only way to get to the origin of morals.

Who is Nietzsche's potential (implied) reader?

A reader is clearly implied in any literary or philosophical work. First, this guarantees that the book would be taken seriously and that the reader would reflect on the book as well. If there would have been no potential reader whatsoever, the literary work might be quite different. That is not to say that there are no philosophers that write 'on the shelf', i.e. who do not expect anyone to read their work. There certainly are some writers like that, but it seems that in this case the potential reader is the writer him/herself, or the people that are very much alike him/her intellectually, emotionally, etc. But this is not Nietzsche's case, of course. Nietzsche does have the idea of his potential reader: a very peculiar one, it appears. The peculiarity of Nietzsche's work is that *it does not matter who the potential reader is*. It is not that he does not care about his reader, but he is by no means interested in making the reader think for himself; he is not trying to 'shake the reader' and let him then decide whether to agree with the author or not. Nietzsche does not leave the decision to the reader; he does not help him to make up his own mind. Nietzsche leads the reader; he expects the reader to follow him and pattern his mind according to what the author says. Nietzsche is manipulating the reader's mind.

It is very important who reads the philosophical work and when. The book itself remains the same throughout the time, but what we usually deal with when reading a philosophical text is not the words themselves, but rather our own interpretation. I am not saying here that there are as many interpretations as there are the readers. But different people tend to see the same things (and texts especially) in a different way. I am sure that we interpret Nietzsche quite differently from the ones who read his book a century ago. Furthermore, we already do have a certain attitude towards Nietzsche's philosophical works — we have set our minds in a certain way — so that we view him and what he has written through the prism of time.

What are 'bad conscience' and 'guilt' for Nietzsche and how does he see punishment in this context? What is the difference between the origin of punishment and its present function?

The concept of guilt is not an old one; it seems to have been introduced to European culture by Christianity. Of course, Christianity itself could not have flourished if the European conscience had not been ready for it, but the pagan "self-assertion" (as Nietzsche writes about it) did not have this clear and distinct notion of guilt. It is indeed an interesting phenomenon that can tell us much. German has the same word for 'guilt' and 'debt'. This is not enough to build a theory on, yet it is tempting to speculate. First, we can derive from this basis that guilt (just like a debt) may be measured. This provides us the notion of justice: it is in principle possible to pay a 'debt' of a different kind. Second, the initial guilt was rather simple in nature; it was not complex as we see 'guilt' now — but that does not tell us much about other kinds of guilt (they might have been out of question).

The guilt in one's mind, as Nietzsche rightly points out, changes one's life, unless it is softened in one way or another. He makes a good point, saying that there could be no happiness, no cheerfulness, no hope, no pride, no *present*, without forgetfulness.[1] This makes a good point: people must forget the negative aspects of their lives (just as they treasure the memories of pleasures), or else their lives would be unbearable. Yet the 'guilt' is meant to be a reminder: it stays there until it is treated properly, and here Nietzsche suggests the notion of punishment. I am not saying that he actually viewed punishment like this and in no other way, but this is one of the possible explanations that seems most plausible. Thus, Nietzsche draws the following scheme:

guilt --- punishment --- forgetfulness --- happiness

According to this view we have to have the punishment as a form of getting rid of the feeling of guilt. The punishment gives us the sense that we have 'paid the debt' and that is why the original guilt is not there any more.

Besides this conception Nietzsche has the following notion of punishment: "man does evil for the pleasure of doing it"[2] and "to see one suffer does one good, to make others suffer even more..."[3] The punishment in itself is an act of suffering or harm (just or unjust) that is applied to the guilty person. The suffering as such does not necessarily have to be the case: it is the power over the one that is helpless and powerless that is important in this case. This is quite an animalistic feeling, for it is power that is gained by virtue of physical force, i.e. it might be unjust. But that suits Nietzsche's theory better. He even refers to man as to 'animal man' throughout the book, for he is talking about man's instincts. Nietzsche also points out that the initial punishment with its passion and function has vanished through the time, so that later on it has become a procedure of justice that measures the suffering according to the guilt.

However, the European conscience can not survive without the feeling of guilt; the man has to punish himself. And Nietzsche says: "the man of bad conscience 'punishes' himself, he drives his self-torture to its most gruesome pitch of severity and rigor..."[4] This man does not have a unified conscience any more. He tears himself into parts and does not know how to deal with them, for they are left conflicting and contradicting one another.[5]

What does Nietzsche object to: 'conscience' or 'the feeling of guilt'?

Nietzsche objects to the feeling of guilt — there is no question about that — yet this is not enough for him. The feeling of guilt does not exist itself; it exists in our conscience. The Christian tradition has left this burden on the conscience of all European peoples. The feeling of guilt itself is not much of a religious feeling, yet it perfectly accords with the Christian tradition. So it is not enough to object to the feeling of guilt itself; the whole conscience appears to be poisoned. It is after all a 'bad conscience' for Nietzsche. And he does not suggest that just some kinds of conscience are bad while others are good. He is challenging the human being as such, as it is and as it became under the burden of the feeling of guilt. Now Nietzsche is anticipating a new type of human being: one that will not be crushed to the ground by the feeling of guilt, the one that will not have the 'conscience'.

Nietzsche's claims remind me of F. Bacon's conception of 'idols': the 'idola tribu' (the idols of the whole of human nature that everyone has just because we all share the same quality, namely, of being human beings). They make us blind. They make us judge about things in a wrong way. They keep us from thinking properly. And there is no way to get rid of them, for if we do not have them, we are not human any more: we simply do not exist.

Nietzsche expresses the same view concerning suffering and the feeling of guilt in one of his aphorisms, where he deals with the meaning of ascetic ideals. There he holds that, according to the ascetic ideal, man was desperately lacking any *meaning* and this lack of meaning made man suffer (yet he was suffering because of other factors as well). The suffering itself came of man: he did not object to it; all he wanted was the meaning of this suffering, the purpose and the goal. The suffering itself was already the ascetic ideal of the mankind, yet that was not enough: the suffering was "placed in the perspective of guilt"; it was well-grounded. And by this man finally obtained his meaning, that is why he *needs* suffering, he also *needs* the feeling of guilt as the ground for it. Thus Nietzsche draws the following scheme again:

search for meaning --- suffering --- guilt --- 'meaning'.

Why did Descartes call his book '*Meditations* on First Philosophy'?

Descartes, Bacon, Leibniz, *et al* tend to start with the very beginning. They themselves are the tradition. They themselves are the measure of the new style and the new thought. That is why Descartes did not refer to any Ancient or Medieval philosophers; he did not cite either Plato, or Aristotle or the Fathers of the Church. He can be hardly said to object to them or ignore them; they are simply beyond his concern, for Descartes himself knows the way in philosophy and his system (now as a part of the tradition and even as a classical example of it) is self-contained, self-sufficient. The 'Meditations' are meant to be not a discourse in philosophy, not an analysis of the former theories; the 'Meditations' are meant to reveal the *inner* self of the philosopher and show what is in his own mind. Descartes 'meditates'; he 'reflects' and in this action he does not need any references to anyone else. The 'Meditations' is a unique example of what a real philosopher can do, not even leaving his chair. Descartes shows his reader that the genuine philosophy is within self and not outside; we have to look inward and not outward to find the truth. On the other hand, this is also the weak point of his philosophy: it is too speculative, it has too little to do with the external world, it rests on the truths that can not be tested elsewise than by the mind itself. But whenever the system is based on reason, it is purely rational and self-dependent.

Although Descartes refers to his method as to 'demonstration', this is purely rational demonstration. (Descartes' terminology was well adopted by later philosophers: the term 'to demonstrate' when talking not about experience but rational evidence, is still widely used).

Who is Descartes' implied reader?

As Descartes himself claims in his 'Letter of Dedication' ("Meditations on First Philosophy'), his book is aimed to prove the existence of God and soul to those who do not believe in it; he says that his proof is so evident that even non-believers would 'see' these self-revealing truths. Yet, it seems, this work was done not to prove these truths to the reader.[6] Like the pure 'meditation', his work was aimed at himself in the first place: he was the one who meditated and he was the one who absorbed the results of the meditation. Besides that, meditation has itself as its own result; its aim does not go beyond that which is being done at the very moment of meditation. The truth that is being revealed is the truth for the one who was meditating in the first place, and only after that is it revealed to anyone else. So Descartes *is himself his first reader*, and the most important one.

Thus, Descartes *does not need* the tradition of philosophy, does not deal with it, and is free from it (though certain aspects of his theory do resemble former traditions). Nietzsche, on the other hand, *needs* tradition: if there were no European tradition, no European history and philosophy in particular, there would have been no Nietzsche. He feeds himself from this source, he needs it to support *his* philosophy as opposed to the whole former one.

Descartes looks inside himself to search for the truth while Nietzsche looks outside, to the world as it formed itself throughout history. Nietzsche is not concerned with truth, he looks for *action* — he looks for the super-being that would prove his theory to be true.[7] And we indeed are the super-being that Nietzsche was expecting to come — we, who have buried God — we who live while God is dead.

In spite of all these differences, Descartes and Nietzsche have something in common: neither needs a reader. Descartes is concerned with his inner self and the inner truth and thus is self-content with that. Nietzsche's theory is good for the sake of the theory itself and does not need any support from outside. And after all, both Descartes and Nietzsche have found their readers, the ones that are willing to perform the same action themselves (whether it is Cartesian meditation or a Nietzschean rejection of former 'prejudices').

NOTES

1. See "On the Genealogy of Morals," page 58.

2. *Ibid.*, p. 65.

3. *Ibid.*, p. 67.

4. *Ibid.*, p. 92.

5. This is what Nietzsche sees as reflection in Christianity. He thinks that the whole conception of self-denying and guilt is erroneous, naturally.

6. I doubt that Descartes assumed that his book would be read by all those who were doubting their religion

7. Here 'super' does not mean 'better', it means 'above' in the sense of 'later'.

REFERENCES

Descartes, Rene. *Meditations on First Philosophy.*

Nietzsche, Friedrich. *The Genealogy of Morals.*

Oneonta

Undergraduate Philosophy Conference

at State University of New York, Oneonta

Host: SUNY Oneonta Philosophy Club

March 16, 1996

Funded by the Student Association, Oneonta Philosophy Studies, and the Ninash Foundation

Bliss and Madness: Varying Views

Chair: Laurence Grisanti

A Method to the Madness
Aaron Hunter (Oneonta)
Commentator: Mike Jablonski

Follow Your Bliss: The Philosophy of Joseph Campbell
Angela Case (Le Moyne College)
Commentator: Tiffany Streeter

Quality, Love, and Madness: Pirsig vs. Plato
Kerri Nicholas (Oneonta)
Commentator: John Costa

Socrates, Descartes, and Nietzsche: Character and Expression

Chair: David Schaaf

Socrates Character Sketch
David T. McCann (Oneonta)
Commentators: Brian Bauder, David Schaaf, and Jonathan Pariot

Descartes and Nietzsche
Tatiana Zelikina (Moscow State and SUNY-Albany)
Commentator: Ben Stedge

Nietzsche's Appropriative Representation or *Is the Overman a Hermaphrodite?*
John D. Devine (Alfred University)
Commentator: Michelle Blemur

Science, Metaphysics, and The Construction of Reality

Chair: Tiffany Streeter

Biological Research and Feminist Obligation
Jennifer Burke (Temple University)
Commentator: Tara Mattarazzo

Subjective vs. Objective Reality: An Examination Through Physics and Philosophy
Michael Joseph (Oneonta)
Commentator: Ian Gartland

Exploring the Universe: From Plato to Einstein and Beyond
Alex Slater (Oneonta)
Commentator: Rich Dyckoff

Observing Observability and the Importance of the Smiler: A Partial Defense of Strawsonian Events
David Miguel Gray (Columbia University)
Commentator: Marilyn Collins

Pirsig and Hesse: Philosophical Journeys

Chair: Beth Mattone

The Search for Universal Truth
Eric Gassick (Oneonta)

My Metaphysical Quest
Justin Mandel (Oneonta)

A Comparison of Narcissus and Goldmund by Hermann Hesse and Zen and The Art of Motorcycle Maintenance by Robert Pirsig
Nathan Smith (Oneonta)

MATTERS OF THE SPIRIT

Chair: Lynn Danielle Braunstein

Keep It to Yourself-Power:
The Importance of Buddhism's Shingon School
Sarah Kalliney (Skidmore College)
Commentator: Anthony Jimenez

Concepts of Self: East and West
Gabrielle Levin (Oneonta)
Commentator: Mary Abigail Thomas

The Mysticism of Chess and Zen
Raymond J. Mollica (Oneonta)
Commentator: Alex Slater

Can One Gain Spiritual Fulfillment Without God or Religion?
Nikolai Schulman (Oneonta)
Commentator: Anthony Jimenez

SUICIDE, SEX, AND KANT

Chair: Melissa Dora Benjamin

Suicide: Why Many People Commit Suicide
and Why Many Other People Don't
Michael Joseph (Oneonta)
Commentators: Lynn Szafranski and Liam Sweeney

To Have Sex or Not to Have Sex? -- That is the Question
Cassandra J. Shultis (Oneonta)
Performers: Cassandra J. Shultis, Kirstin Connelly, and Beth Mattone
Commentator: Kirstin Connelly

The Impossibilities, Irrationality, and Contradictions of Immanuel Kant's Ethical Theories
David Schaaf (Oneonta)
Commentator: John Costa

AWARDS CEREMONY AND KEYNOTE ADDRESS

Imaginative Cosmology from Plato to Einstein
Thomas M. Robinson (University of Toronto)

Brief Biography

Education: Universities of Durham, Oxford, and Paris

Current Post: Professor of Philosophy and Classics
University of Toronto

Major Publications:
Plato's Psychology (first edition 1970, second 1975)
Contrasting Arguments: An Edition of the Dissoi Logoi (1979)
The Greek Legacy (1979)
Heraclitus: Fragments. A Text and Translation with a Commentary (1987)

Major Editorial Work:
Editor, *Phoenix* (1971-1978)
Co-editor, *The Phoenix Presocratic Series* (1978-)

Other:
Chairman, Department of Philosophy University of Toronto (1979-1981)
Dean, School of Graduate Studies University of Toronto (1984-1989)
President, Canadian Federation for the Humanities (1988-1990)
President, Society for Ancient Greek Philosophy (1993-1995)
President, International Plato Society (1995-present)
Honorary President, International Association for Greek Philosophy (1993-present)

Reception (9:00 - 11:00 p.m.)

Oneonta Philosophy Studies

Historical and Cultural Perspectives

Oneonta Philosophy Studies is a scholarly series which promotes exchange concerning traditional and contemporary issues in philosophy. Because comparative study often fosters appreciation and tolerance as well as understanding, special consideration is given to manuscripts which illuminate relationships between diverse or seemingly discrete views. Historical and cultural studies are especially welcome.

Submission is open to all — without regard to institutional affiliation, political preference, religious belief, gender, or national origin. Manuscripts are subject to external review. Published material does not necessarily reflect the views of the Editorial Board, the Philosophy Department, or the State University of New York.

A series such as this depends on the vision, good will, and labor of many. Special appreciation is extended to the *Institute of Global Cultural Studies* (IGCS), *Society for Ancient Greek Philosophy* (SAGP), *Society for the Study of Islamic Philosophy and Science* (SSIPS), and the State University of New York at Oneonta — especially James Mullen (Dean of Humanities and Fine Arts, now retired), Anne Cairns Federlein (Provost and Vice President for Academic Affairs) and Alan B. Donovan (President).

Douglas W. Shrader
Editor in Chief

Books

• Virtue, Order, Mind:
Ancient, Modern, and Post-Modern Perspectives
Peter Vincent Amato, editor

On Choosing a Teacher: Plato's *Protagoras* (MARIE I. GEORGE); Words of Love: Rhetoric and Eros in Plato's *Phaedrus* (DOUGLAS W. SHRADER); Tragic *Katharsis* (MARTHA HUSAIN); *Metaphysics* Z and H: Spurious V. Genuine Genera (WALTER E. WEHRLE); Aquinas, Aristotle, and the Convertibility of Being and Truth (JAMES T. H. MARTIN); Toxic Shame and the Lonerganian Concept of Conversion (DENNIS D. KLEIN); Jonas on the Crisis for Modern Man (OSCAR MOHL AND ANGELO JUFFRAS); A Roadmap for Ethics in the Twenty-First Century (EDDY SOUFFRANT); Communicative Rationality, Communicative Ethics and the Political Space of the Public Sphere (EVANGELOS KOBOLAKIS); A Pragmatic Reading of Gadamer's Philosophical Hermeneutics (VINCENT MARK VACCARO); Reconceiving Power and the Social Through Baudrillard (MARC HANES); A Feminist Analysis of Value-Neutral Observation (MAUREEN LINKER); Modernity, Kolakowski and Myth (PETER VINCENT AMATO).
1994 — 203 pages — ISBN 1-883058-16-3

• Essays in Islamic Philosophy, Theology, and Mysticism,
Parviz Morewedge

Basic Dimensions of Islamic Theology; Basic Concepts of Neoplatonism; Greek Sources of Some Islamic Philosophies of Being and Existence; Substance and Process Theories of the Self in Islamic Mysticism; Mystical Icons in Rumi's Metaphysical Poetry: Light, the Mediator and the Way; Sufism, Neoplatonism and Zaehner's Theistic Theory of Mysticism.
1995 — 265 + xxviii pages — ISBN 0-9633277-7-1

• Jean Paul Sartre's Existentialism in Literature and Philosophy
Ashok Kumar Malhotra

This book offers innovative approaches to the reading of the novel *Nausea*, considering it as a philosophical and a psychological novel, and as a work of art. After depicting the existential themes in *Nausea*, the author compares the existential philosophy of *Nausea* to that of *Being and Nothingness*, and then deals with the ethical and social dimensions of Sartre's philosophy before exploring the interconnection between philosophy, art, and literature.
1995 — 154 + x pages — ISBN 1-883058-14-7

• Seeds of Wisdom
Douglas W. Shrader, editor

Biological Research and Feminist Obligation (JENNIFER BURKE); Subjective versus Objective Reality: An Examination Through Physics and Philosophy (MICHAEL JOSEPH); Exploring the Universe: From Plato to Einstein and Beyond (ALEX SLATER); Observing, Observability, and the Importance of a Smiler: A Partial Defense of Strawsonian Events (DAVID MIGUEL GRAY); Follow Your Bliss: The Philosophy of Joseph Campbell (ANGELA CASE); Concepts of Self: East and West (GABRIELLE LEVIN); Quality, Love, and Madness: Pirsig versus Plato (KERRI NICHOLAS); Nietzsche's Appropriative Representation *or* Is the Overman a Hermaphrodite? (JOHN DEVINE); The Impossibilities, Irrationality, and Contradictions of Immanuel Kant's Ethical Theories (DAVID SCHAAF); Descartes and Nietzsche (TATIANA ZELIKINA)
1997 — 167 + xii pages — ISBN 1-883058-08-2

Research Papers

• **The Logic Beneath the Caution: An Analysis of the Buddha's Responses to Questions About the Self**
Douglas W. Shrader
1992 — 22 pages — ISBN 0-9633277-3-9

• **On Hindu Philosophies of Experience: Cults, Mysticism, and Meditations**
Ashok K. Malhotra
1993 — 75 pages — ISBN 1-883058-03-1

• **Near-Death Experiences: Scientific, Philosophical, and Religious Perspectives**
Douglas W. Shrader
1995 — 56 pages — ISBN 0-9633277-9-8

Department of Philosophy
SUNY-ONEONTA
Oneonta, NY 13820-4015

HTTP://WWW.ONEONTA.EDU/~SHRADEDW/OPS.HTML